La Vie Est Belle

Learning to live hopefully ever after

Vie Portland

VieNess Discover You Love You CIC

Printed in the United Kingdom
First Printing, 2021

ISBN: 978-1-8384274-4-3 (Paperback)
ISBN: 978-1-8384274-5-0 (eBook)

VieNess Discover You Love You CIC
Southampton, Hants
SO40 4WU

Contents

Chapter One

La Vie Est Belle: Learning to live hopefully ever after

There are always three versions of any story: my story, your story, and the truth. This is my story, the story I have lived. There will be others who disagree because they don't want to be remembered this way.

Sometimes I wonder how different my life would have been had I had a loving, encouraging, family who believed in me. Then I remind myself how far I have come, by learning to believe in myself, and I am grateful I am me.

Chapter Two

A short story

"You cannot protect yourself from sadness without protecting yourself from happiness." — *Jonathan Safran Foer*

A little girl called Vie.

Once upon a time a baby girl was born. As the first born, she was expected to look after younger siblings, both by birth and fostered, while also protecting them from a narcissistic mother and emotionally absent father. The little girl was told she was only good for looking after people more stupid than she was.

She grew up thinking she was useless and unlovable. She went into jobs where she often wasn't considered important, and she went into relationships that confirmed how useless and unlovable she was.

She got very, very sad; her body was very sore because no one had cared enough to get her to a good doctor when she was little, even though she often had inexplicable wounds. And her head was very broken because she had believed all the bad things people had said.

Then, around 14 or so years ago, she felt so very sad that she started looking for ways to not be living anymore. It was very, very sad. Thankfully, she had a new best friend: a tiny little kitten that was thrown out of her family for being too small. The two of them knew that no one loved the other as much as they loved each other, so they decided to work very hard together to try to find happiness. The girl shut all the mean people out of her life and started finding things to do that might make her happy.

She had always loved to dance, but it was always something her mean parents told her to do alone because she was too fat and too ugly to be seen by anyone else. She decided now was the time to try something different. She had already been close to death a couple of times, so she knew that no matter how bad she was, she wasn't going to die from it.

She found a burlesque class! Oh my! That was a challenge! But she loved it! And people told her she was good at it! She was good at something! Her heart warmed up a little.

On a dare, she performed alone once, thinking people would be horrible. They weren't! And, from that once only performance, she went on to become an international performer! People loved her! They loved her so much, they wanted her to teach them! Her heart warmed some more.

She tried vintage inspired clothes, clothes she had always loved, and decided to go to vintage dances. People saw her dance and asked her to teach them! The girl was baffled but very pleased. Soon, people began saying that the girl was changing lives through her teaching, by encouraging them to see how wonderful they are, because she now knew how important it was to hear honest kindness; she had also been talking to herself far more kindly for a while; those people asked her to teach them how to feel happier with who they are. And she did. And she does. And she continues to live hopefully ever after helping people find their happy ever after.

Chapter Three

Tears

"Tears are words that need to be written." — Paulo Coelho

It's important that every child feels loved and secure. It's important that every adult feels the same. Unfortunately, this is not always the case.

For some, childhood can be a horrific time, full of scary and upsetting things. Those children may not react to some things in the same way that others do. Sometimes, those reactions carry on until adulthood. Those behaviours can be limiting to their lives. They may find it hard to love, themselves or others. They may develop relationships that aren't healthy for them. They may develop habits that cause damage.

I was one of those children. I grew up with a couple of addicts in my extended family, so I watched and learned what not to do. Thankfully, I didn't become an addict. However, I had a few very unhealthy relationships that were incredibly damaging, and I developed coping techniques that were harmful. I locked a lot of myself away, not knowing how to interact and be safe. I didn't like who I was, or how I looked, because I so rarely heard words of unconditional love. I was too frequently criticised, too frequently told I was worthless, and, like all children, I believed what the adults who were meant to love me told me.

Because I had grown up in a damaging environment, where I was told my only value was in doing things for others, it was natural for me to be working in roles where I was caring, so I worked for many years — as a nanny, in schools, in after school groups, and summer schemes — with children from birth to 19. I knew deep inside that I couldn't repeat the way I was brought up, so from very early on, I was always who I had needed when I was growing up. I wasn't going to repeat damaging behaviours, instead choosing to demonstrate the love and encouragement I never received. I just didn't know how to show love and encouragement to myself.

I worked with so many wonderful children; I taught them many things, and they taught me too. I encouraged learning of all subjects; it was never a chore; it was always something that could be fun. I encouraged acceptance of all different people and of themselves. I encouraged kindness. I talked about it, and I demonstrated it, even though I couldn't accept who I was and wasn't kind to myself.

Then I reached a point where I knew my choices were bleak. I couldn't carry on the way I was. I knew things either had to end, stay the same, or I had to make changes. As you are here, reading my book, you know I am not a ghost (takes ghost writing to a whole new level!). Hopefully, you have realised that I made big changes. I learned ways to love who I am, as I am, with no pressure to be anyone else.

I haven't written this book chronologically; it felt like that would be too much, both for me and you, the reader, to work through almost four decades of sadness, hurt and pain. I want to show you the things I have lived through, almost subject by subject, rather than year by year, and, and in the second part of the book, give you hope that things can and do change. There, I'll give you an insight into how I changed, and how you can, if you want to.

I'm not going to say change is easy, because it often isn't. I am going to say it's nearly always worth it, though. And I hope you read this book, see what I have overcome, and believe that you, that anyone who is open to it, can find the happier life they want.

There are some deeply emotional topics here. Please keep yourself safe when you read about them. At no point think, "What she went through was far worse than me so I shouldn't be as upset/concerned/freaked by what happened to me" or that I went through less than you, so I couldn't possibly understand. One trauma is enough trauma for anyone, and we all deserve love, kindness, and respect. Be kind to yourself. There are numbers and websites at the back of the book if you feel you need additional support.

Before we go any further, I would like you to write on a Post-it note or a piece of paper, or even on the inside cover of this book, these words:

I deserve love.

I deserve respect.

I deserve kindness.

Read them frequently. Believe them.

Vie

xx

Chapter Four

My family love

"Family love is messy, clinging, and of an annoying and repetitive pattern, like bad wallpaper." — Friedrich Nietzsche

Living back in the city of my childhood was never part of the plan.

Growing up (mostly) there, I hated it. I was desperate to leave and experience more of the things I wanted to explore.

However, in hindsight, it wasn't the city that was at fault; it was my limited experiences of it and the people I met.

So, how did I end up back there?

It certainly wasn't an easy route.

I had to take a year out of university because I failed one subject; my partner at the time (Tom)[1] and I moved to London, and I did temporary nanny jobs. One of the families was especially wonderful and, in my final year, although I was back in the West Country, working as a live-in nanny, and doing my studies, I commuted back to London for two days a week so I could continue working for them for a few more months. I left to focus on the final few months of my degree, and I thought I wouldn't be a nanny again. I thought people would be queueing at my door to employ a graduate. That didn't happen.

After being tempted back to London to work with my favourite family again, I left them after a couple of years; I left partly because I was so unhappy with myself, and so stressed about money, that I thought a change would be good, that a change would solve things. But I was trying to run away from the real issues that I couldn't run away from, because they were living inside me.

I went from my favourite family to the worst family. I knew very soon that I had made a mistake. The dad was okay, but the mother was awful; from the start, she was cruel and unreasonable. I thought I just needed to prove I was worthy of the job. I had a lifetime of experience of trying to prove I was worthy, so this wasn't a new feeling.

She didn't work, so she was around a lot of the time. The two older children, especially the eldest, struggled with this. They couldn't understand why they had to have someone look after them when their mother was always around.

The mother loved to undermine me at every opportunity. She would tell me to ensure the children ate all of their main course before they were allowed dessert, and then she would come in at mealtimes and tell them they didn't have to eat it and that I was just mean. She would ask me to arrange playdates, then tell me to cancel them, before arranging the same playdate at the same time, and telling the parents/nanny of the other family that it was me, saying I didn't want the children to play. She would tell me to play particular educational games with them, then she would come in and say how boring they were and ask why on earth was I making them play them.

They would frequently talk about their BEST NANNY EVER, telling me how much better than me she was, how they would have her back if ever she was looking for work again. She had left because she was moving in with her boyfriend and this family wanted live-in help.

It was the weekend of the eldest child's birthday. The week preceding, I got told the BEST NANNY EVER was looking for work again, but that she didn't have plans to come back to this family; it still unsettled me.

On the Saturday, I had arranged to take the eldest child into the centre of London; they were a wealthy family and the children had everything they needed, so I suggested an experience, which the parents agreed to; she and I went to a children's play at a theatre, to lunch wherever she wanted, and then we went to look around Hamley's, the famous toy shop; we had a lovely day.

On the Sunday, I hosted her birthday party, including preparing for it and cleaning up after it. I didn't get paid for any of my time. I just felt it would show my dedication; I had also worked other Sundays, unpaid, for their other family events, so I felt this was expected.

On the Monday morning, I had dropped the eldest at school, the middle one at nursery, and the baby was sleeping while I started to prepare dinner. The mother came into the kitchen and asked me to sit down with her.

She then sat and told me vile things she had been told about me. Apparently, the oldest daughter had said I had pushed the baby down the stairs; I was horrified, I would never, ever do that! She also said that several of my nanny peers had told her that I yelled at the children and told them I hated them. I have very rarely ever raised my voice — I have always found that children are more likely to stop if you get quieter, as they're curious about what you are saying; and the only people I have said I hated were my siblings in childhood fights. The one peer who stayed loyal to me said that the mother had paid the other nannies to say those things. I was devastated.

Then, the mother told me that I only ever worked when I was getting paid and never a second more; I tried to argue about all the weekends I had worked with no payment, including the one we had just had, all the extra evenings I babysat (I was contracted to do two a week, but they would frequently go out more, as "you're going to be in anyway"), but I was so distraught I just couldn't get the words out through the tears.

When she had finished telling me all these awful things, which devastated me, being the polite and dutiful carer I was, I asked if I should finish cooking the dinner before I started packing, she responded, "Well, yes! That's the one thing you do well!"

In the space of an hour, I had lost my job and my home. I had no clue what to do. I phoned my favourite family; they were wonderful! Reassuring me that they knew none of those things were true; reassuring me that I had over a decade's worth of experience showing how great I was. Then I phoned a friend, and she said I could sleep on their sofa until I found a new job, which was lovely of them.

The thing is, I was too scared to return to nannying. I knew I wasn't the person they were claiming I was, but I was so scared that people disliked me so much that they would believe them. To tell me I was abusive to children, after the childhood I had had, after dedicating much of my life to the safety and well-being of children, I was devastated.

I didn't want to outstay my welcome, so I asked my mum if I could return and stay with her for a few weeks, until I found a new job. It was the last thing I wanted to do — I had said I would never live in my home city again — but I felt I had no choice. So I moved back and into the tiny spare room at my mum's and her then husband's.

As expected, it was awful. My step-father was shorter than me, and not particularly bright, so he would often try to belittle me, cornering me in the kitchen, testing me on things he thought I should know the answers to, including creating bizarre emergency situations where I would be the only first aider on site. My first aid qualifications had always been around children; oddly, what I would do in a situation where I was at the docks, a large cable had broken and landed in a large, deep, puddle, and a man was dangling from a crane, 30 feet up, had not come up in the many classes I had attended. I had always found him quite idiotic, though, so it never troubled me; I was baffled why my mum was with him though.

The few months I was with them were difficult. As always, when around my mum, I was on an emotional roller coaster: the constant need for her approval; the ever present concern that she was going to yell at me; the inconsistencies in her behaviour and words. Over the years, she and I had written many letters to each other, usually in reaction to an argument; many times she had accused me of wanting to be better than her and my sisters, and I would say I just wanted something different, that it was okay to want to develop on what had come before. She would tell me I would never be as good as my sisters, that I was a failure. Living back with her, she frequently raised the issue of me being a failure, having to move back in with my parents. One time, she threw me out, and told me she never wanted to see me again; gratefully, friends said I could move in with them for a while. My mum then went around telling everyone that I was ungrateful, and I had stormed out.

Two weeks later, I moved back. Again, I didn't want to outstay my welcome at my friends'.

I had been struggling to find work, but finally, I had found work at a summer scheme for children and young people, and I had been offered a job as a Learning Support Assistant at a secondary school. I told my mum and said that I would be looking for somewhere to move to, so I was "out of her hair" as soon as possible.

"Look for somewhere with two bedrooms. I'm leaving your step-father (she always called him by his name, so I felt she used this to add to the drama) and I am moving in with you."!!!

The panic! The thoughts going around in my head! Had she finally accepted me? Unlikely. Did she want to continue to torment me? Almost definitely. Was she using me as an excuse to leave him? Yes. Would we get on better if it was just the two of us? Doubtful.

But I didn't feel I could say no, and my overwhelming need to be accepted by her meant that I felt I had to do this.

So I started looking for a two bedroom flat. When I found somewhere, she didn't tell my step-dad she was leaving; she told him she was giving me stuff for the new place, and that she had been meaning to clear her wardrobes for a while. He found out when she just wasn't there one day when he got home from work.

She picked the biggest bedroom, obviously. She said it was because it was near the kitchen, and she liked to get up early for a coffee. She said we would need a freezer. Because there was no room for one in the kitchen, she would "have to" have it in her room, and always playing the martyr, she would learn to "cope with" the noise of it.

I had the smallest room, though still a good size, down the hallway.

Even though I had found the flat, even though it was meant to be her moving in with me, even though it was a lovely flat, it never felt like mine.

Part of it was that she always decided when we were having people over; although a bonus was that my nieces, her grandchildren, both little at the time, came to stay frequently. Another part of it was that, whenever she had a day off, if she didn't have plans to fill every moment of her day, I would come home to furniture and other things having been moved around (interestingly, although I found it unsettling, I didn't realise quite how much until, after moving into a house with my partner, many years later; he thought he would surprise me by rearranging the lounge while I was out; I came home, saw it, and had a panic attack. My brain told me that he was changing the room to remind me that it wasn't my home. It scared me so much. I thought he was telling me our relationship was over. I know it was irrational, but it was a gut reaction — the panic was terrifying. He has never done it again).

And a huge part of the problem with living with my mum was that I was never sure what mood she was going to be in, so I could never relax. There were lots of arguments, followed by lots of silences. I'm not sure which was worse: her yelling at me, telling me how crap I was, or being in the silence, thinking about how crap I was and waiting for the yelling to start again. I felt I had reverted to childhood; so scared of the yelling and the horrible things she said, but more scared of the silences and terrified of what was to come.

Childhood. I can honestly say I would struggle to remember ten happy moments from childhood with my family.

You'll hear about other parts of my unhappy childhood in other chapters, but, as I am telling you about the relationship with my mum, I thought I would add in just a few of the things she did.

One of my earliest memories is of being in the bathroom with my sister: I was a toddler, and she was a baby. We had been left there while my mum went off to do something (I don't know what, get a nappy, answer the phone; I don't know). My sister accidentally knocked over a bottle of talcum powder on herself. We thought it was funny. My mum came back and yelled at me because I hadn't looked after my sister properly. Then she yelled at me some more when my sister started to cry.

"How dare you make your sister cry?!!"

My mum would regularly criticise me in front of everyone, including my friends. To everyone else, she was great, lovely, friendly, the "cool" mum. On the rare occasion friends came over, she would be ever so nice to them, and then say things like:

"Well, we all know [birth name] is boring."

Or…

"Ignore her. You'll have more fun playing with her sisters anyway."

As an adult, I know that my friends probably didn't want to disagree with a grown-up; as a child, it hurt so much that they did what she asked.

When we were out, she liked to humiliate me. One time, we were in a high street store; it was me, my mum, and my youngest sister. At the time, my youngest sister was a few sizes bigger than me. As the two of them were pondering over something to buy my sister, I wandered off to look around the rest of the shop. I was on the other side of the shop when she shouted: "[Birth name], these should fit your fat arse!"

I was frequently told how fat and ugly I was. The first time I remember it happening was in my maternal grandmother's kitchen. My nan's twin was looking at photos from an auntie's wedding; my middle sister and I had been bridesmaids. In the kitchen were my "great" auntie, my nan, my mum, her two sisters, and my sister. My "great" aunt slowly went through the photos, and then she turned to me and said:

"Such a shame you're so fucking ugly and not pretty like your sister."

Everyone laughed. I was about 6 years old.

Things were much the same as I grew older. Mum continued to try to be the "bestie" of my friends, and when I started having boyfriends, she came on to all of them. She would sidle up to them in the kitchen and casually brush past them with her breasts; at parties, when she was usually drunk, she would slow dance with them and tell them they were wasting their time with me, and that she was a far better lover than I would ever be. Because I was, mostly, not very good at picking boyfriends, they enjoyed the attention and loved to gloat about it. So did she.

All of these things, and the many more memories I have of her, are great examples of narcissistic behaviour. I didn't know that then because narcissists are brilliant at making their scapegoat feel like everything is their fault.

Back to sharing the flat together.

I don't know what made me think it but, one day, I realised that she got enjoyment from me being miserable, that she loved the reactions she got from me, that they made her feel powerful. So I decided I wasn't going to react the way she expected me to.

The first time I put my plan to the test, she was standing in the hallway, in between her bedroom door and the kitchen, and I was stood in the doorway of my bedroom. I can't remember what she had decided this argument was about; I was too busy trying to pretend I was calm.

She started yelling at me.

I smiled.

She yelled louder.

I continued to smile.

She got louder and more verbally aggressive.

"Go on," I said, in a very sweet, overly encouraging tone. "I know it makes you happy to try to make me miserable. I know you like to tell me how crap I am. Go on. Get it all out." I did this with an encouraging arm movement, as if I was in an American sitcom, saying, "Go on, Sport! You got this!"

I kept repeating this as she continued yelling. Then I watched as she deflated and went into the kitchen.

I went into my bedroom and sobbed. I was smiling at her, but inside, she had torn open all the wounds that never got the chance to heal.

We did this one more time, and then she never shouted at me again. Things didn't get easier, but at least they weren't so loud.

She started seeing a new man. He was okay; too chauvinistic for my liking, but he was of the era they grew up in, so she was fine with it.

Quite quickly, they decided to move in together.

There was no gentleness, no consideration of what I was going to do. I couldn't afford to stay in the flat on my own, and she knew that, but she didn't care; she was moving and that was my problem.

I moved into a tiny little flat on my own. I loved that flat! It was closer to my new job, and it was in a lovely part of the city. I painted the hallway and lounge/kitchen a bright sunny yellow. I wanted it to represent the sunnier times I hoped to have. It felt safe, too. The same as when I was living in the flat in London that my favourite family let me live in as part of tempting me back, I felt safer alone. Not surprising, really, when I had suffered so much at the hands of others. I didn't feel safe elsewhere, practically nowhere, but in my cosy little flat, I felt at home.

The new job. For the first time, I felt like I had a "grown-up" job because I was working in an office. I'm really not suited to office work. And, at the time (at any time?) I was not suited to working for a dominant boss that took delight in bullying anyone whom she perceived as a threat, for reasons only known to her. I believed she picked on me because she knew I had no confidence; I didn't do things her way and she criticised me. Because I was very new to office work, I was very much learning as I went along but that was not good enough. My passion for the organisation and for the people we supported was not good enough. Even when I did things exactly the way she wanted, it was never good enough, as she delighted in telling me in nearly every team meeting: berating is always better in front of an audience, it seems.

My mental health had been a consistent struggle, but I had always managed to put up a good facade; now, that facade was crumbling.

Being close to my family again, being reminded how worthless they thought I was, fearing bumping into other family members every time I left my home, being bullied at work, feeling out of my depth, having huge money issues from simply living as a single person on a small wage — it was all too much. I was close to breaking, and my self-harming was getting worse.

End of chapter note: If any of this has affected you, there are details of organisations in the back of the book that may help. Please take care of you.

---

1. All names have been changed to protect the privacy of those being discussed.

Chapter Five

Difficult people

"I am thankful for all those difficult people in my life. They have shown me exactly who I do not want to be." — *Al. E Gater*

It was a Wednesday when I heard that an uncle had died, via text message.

Not just an "uncle"; he was my first abuser.

When you have been abused, it's normal to have revenge fantasies, and it's normal to have fantasies of confronting them and them saying they were very wrong and how sorry they were.

With that text message, that all died too. I would never get the apology. It added to my worthlessness. I did not deserve an apology. I did not even deserve to be told in person.

And, sat at my corner desk, I had a panic attack.

The lovely woman I shared the office with helped me to the building's lounge; another lovely colleague held my hand; another made me a hot drink (thankfully, the boss was out for the day). All I could say, over and over, was,

"My uncle is dead."

They took my tears as sadness at a loved one dying. I couldn't tell them otherwise, but hearing them say how wonderful he must have been to have me in tears like this cut into me so deeply. Inside I felt like I was screaming, incandescent with rage, listing all the abuses I'd suffered at his hands; outside, I was a quivering, sobbing mess, struggling to breathe, struggling to be understood.

When my breathing had settled, I left to go home.

The thing with panic attacks is that they can be mortifying. Not only are the physical aspects of it painful and exhausting, but if you have an audience, the embarrassment can be mammoth. Nobody wants to be seen heaving, sobbing, snot-covered, and incomprehensible, especially not in front of your colleagues.

The next couple of days after the news, I barely stopped shaking, and I cried hourly.

I returned to work on my birthday, two days later; a colleague was leaving, and I wanted to be there to say goodbye; and, always concerned about what others thought, I also didn't want to be accused of skiving and being tight. I had to be there to take cakes in.

My boss called me into her office. At first, she seemed kind; I wondered if I had got her wrong. Then she told me how awful it was for me to decide to (yes, "decide to"!) have a panic attack at work and how distressing it was for my colleagues; it was inconsiderate of me to put them in that position. Down I went another notch on how worthless it was possible to feel.

I saw through the day; laughed with my colleagues; that evening I celebrated with friends; that weekend, I cried, and I cried, and, for good measure, I cried some more.

On the Monday, I got signed off from work for two weeks, which became a month, three months, forever.

End of chapter note: I hope you are okay. There are some especially harrowing chapters coming up; please go carefully and look after yourself. There are organisations listed in the back of the book that may be able to help if you feel you need to talk.

Chapter Six

Without protection

"The predator can always tell who is without protection." —
Gabor Matē

I should explain more about the uncle, as that's relevant to this part of the story.

He was one of my dad's older brothers. He was never diagnosed but everyone called him "special". He wasn't particularly bright, and he could barely read or write (all the brothers were dyslexic, so this was an issue for all of them), but he had a steady job and paid bills at my grandparents' house, where he lived most of his life.

We had moved away from the city for a couple of years, and we were moving back. Until we found somewhere else to live, we were staying with my maternal grandparents, and my paternal grandparents were storing our belongings.

I was 8 years old.

Dad had hired a van to move our furniture in. He parked it at the top of the bank that my grandparents lived at the bottom of. After many trips up and down the steps, I asked if I could get in the back of the van; I had never been inside one before, so I wanted to see what it was like. My uncle was in there, sorting stuff to hand out to my parents.

As soon as my dad took another load, my uncle beckoned to me to come stand by him; he had something to show me behind the furniture. I obediently went. He told me to look towards the hatch all the time, because this was our secret, so I had to say when I saw another grown-up. I obediently did as he said. He told me to be quiet because this had to be a quiet thing. I obediently listened. I always tried to be a good girl; I was so desperate for love that I felt that, if I was as good as I could be, then I would be worth loving.

Then he started groping me. He started playing with my back, then my bottom, and then his hand started to go between my legs.

I was quiet, but I was crying. I was scared and didn't like what he was doing, but I was taught that adults always had to be listened to, and that I always had to do what they said. So I stood there, and I didn't make a sound, and I didn't move as the tears and the snot dripped down my face and onto my t-shirt.

And then my dad came back. My uncle whispered:

"This was your fault. You made me do it."

My dad asked why I was crying, and I told him it was because I was scared in the van; he told me I was stupid to be scared of a van; then my mum saw my t-shirt and told me off for not using a tissue and what a dirty girl I was.

I was a dirty girl. I was stupid. It was my fault.

There were several of us children in the family, siblings, cousins. We never talked about him, but we all knew we had to avoid that uncle. At family gatherings, the children would go to the toilet in threes; one to use the loo and two to stand outside together, because we knew we should never be alone.

We all heard so many times: "He [uncle] is just a bit slow, but he's harmless."

He didn't feel harmless to us, but what did we know? We were only children after all.

I spent most weekends at my paternal grandparents' house — the house my uncle also lived in, over the following three years. In that house, I suffered horrible things, but I kept going back because I had a purpose: I had to protect my nan. I took so much in order to protect her, yet I continued to avoid that uncle.

And there were so many horrific things in that house. Logic would ask why I kept going back. Circumstances would say I had no choice.

I was already feeling like I wasn't wanted by my parents.

My middle sister is only 14 months younger than me, so I don't remember a time before her, but right from the start, I knew I had to look after her. I would be told that it was my job. Lots of parents say things like that to their children; it helps encourage a nurturing role between siblings. However, I would be told it was my only job: looking after her was the only point of me.

Then my parents started fostering, and my job was to look after them. In later years, as an adult, my dad told me that they deliberately always had foster children younger than me so that I could look after them. My entire purpose was to care for others.

Then, just before I turned 8, my youngest sister was born, and I had to look after her too. We had a week off school when she was born because dad had returned to

work and mum couldn't walk us to school. We returned to school on my birthday.

As I walked into the classroom, my teacher said, "What a lovely birthday gift! You must be so excited!"

I was impressed with how clever she was, that she knew how excited I was at my fantastic birthday gift! That's why she was a teacher, obviously! I proudly stretched out my left arm and showed her my new Timex blue Snoopy watch with moving arms!

Her face fell, and she said,

"I meant your sister. She's the gift!"

I felt hurt and stupid. I loved my watch but how stupid of me not to realise that it would be my sister who was considered the present. The thing is, I hadn't asked for another sibling, another child to care for, but I had asked for a watch.

While we lived in this town, a hundred or so miles away from our extended family, we didn't see them often. I remember wonderful times playing with friends on the estate. I remember the Silver Jubilee street party. I remember taking photos with a borrowed camera. I know I didn't feel good about who I was, as I was so often reminded about how fat, ugly, and useless I was, but I knew I was good at looking after other people.

So, when my paternal grandparents came to visit, it's no surprise that I loved the attention they gave to just me. They were the only ones that didn't give me jobs to do. They were the only ones who were interested in what I had to say. They always bought me nicer gifts than my sisters. They were the only ones that made me, just me, feel special.

Our other grandfather was amazing! He loved us all! He is still the only person who I feel has loved me unconditionally, and I still miss him, 25 years on from his death. That man believed we, including me, could do whatever we set our minds to. When I was considering going to university to be a teacher, not only was he so proud that I was the first girl in the family to go to university, but he also just knew I was going to change the world. I didn't believe it, but he never doubted it.

It would be hard for me to come up with many happy memories with my family, but there is one event that meant so much to me.

When I was around 15, I was quite good at hurdling; I wasn't particularly fast, but I have long legs so that helped. I would often practise at the local park. However, those hurdles were made of steel and were cemented into the ground; they also weren't regulation width apart. One evening, I was at the park with two friends, and I was practising. The first time over them, I wasted energy by going too high, so I decided to lower my legs the second time round. The front of my ankle caught the first hurdle, and I fell into the second hurdle, then I landed in a heap on the floor with both legs over the first hurdle and my face being very intimate with the concrete. My glasses had broken, and the right lens had cut my cheek; the steel hurdle had broken my cheekbone; and my face was smooshy from the ground.

I got taken to A & E.

I know this doesn't sound like a happy memory yet.

The day it happened was my maternal grandfather's birthday and, for the first time, he was having a birthday party; it was his 70th.

He left his party and sat with me at the hospital.

I felt so guilty, but he kept telling me he would rather be with me then than anywhere else.

We did get to the party, and he acted as my bodyguard all night.

I think that was one of the very few times in my childhood that I felt loved.

His love was incredible. But it was split between his children, their partners, and all of us grandchildren. And my other grandparents seemed to only love me. In a home where I didn't feel loved, where I was only wanted to do things for others, it was so good to feel loved for who I was.

As a child, I thought they were loving me. In hindsight, they were grooming me.

When we moved back to the city, my little sister was still a baby. It seemed that my sister and I were sent somewhere every weekend. My sister would get asked to stay by my aunties; she would get to play with our older, lots of fun, cousins; she would get taken on day trips. When my little sister was older, she got to join them. They never asked me. I felt it was because they didn't like me; that's always the impression my parents gave, but I don't know.

And I always got sent to my paternal grandparents.

My grandfather was a despicable human on all accounts.

When his sons were children, he was a policeman. When they saw him approaching the house, they would prefer to risk broken limbs, jumping from the bedroom windows, rather than have him hit them with his thick leather belt for some indiscretion he thought they had done (he kept that belt on the back of the kitchen door until he died, many years later; a symbol of the fear he could still place in his sons).

My grandmother was a small woman. At the age of eight, I was already as tall as her. She was a recovering alcoholic and a heavy smoker. I remember family parties where my grandfather would invite his workmates (he was no longer a policeman but working in a refinery). He would entice her to drink more and more, then encourage her to strip. He would never buy her her own underwear, so she would be there, dancing, waving her dress above her head, dressed only in his off-white briefs and vest.

When she had surgery to get clean, my parents and I went to visit her in the hospital. The hospital seemed very old fashioned, and I remember this very small human in a very large bed, in a room with heavy wooden doors. She was still groggy from sedation and her only words of wisdom I ever remember her telling me were,

"Always wash your belly button [my birth name]! Mine was disgusting when they took it out!"

I know now that it was highly unlikely she ever saw her removed belly button, but those words of wisdom have stayed with me, and my belly button is incredibly clean.

She did give words of warning, though. She would tell me how to melt toothpaste and boot polish down to get the alcohol out of it; then she would tell me to never need a drink that bad. As a teenager, I realised that I only wanted to drink when I was sad, and, remembering her words, I stopped drinking.

The last time I was drunk, I was 15, and my parents got me drunk (I was "more fun" that way apparently). I was a highly anxious human, but I hated the smell of smoke, knew I couldn't drink, but needed something to do with my hands to occupy them when I was sitting down in a club, so I found little kits I could carry in my handbag. I am quite possibly the only person who has ever tried to do cross stitch in a nightclub.

After her surgery, my grandmother was told never to drink again. She did really well. She did incredibly well when you consider that my evil grandfather always kept a full bar in their conservatory. He also told her that her many Christmas Snowballs were non-alcoholic. He enjoyed the power, but he enjoyed watching her weaknesses even more. And I hated that bloody conservatory! The plastic pineapple on the bar; the terrifying Toby jugs hanging around the room; the smell of stale alcohol and smoke.

And the fact it was a room I was frequently cornered in.

End of chapter note: Are you okay? This might be a good time to do something nice for yourself before you go on to the next chapter, because that one is also harrowing.

Chapter Seven

Forgetting herself

"She tried so hard to make everyone happy, but she realized she was forgetting someone: herself." — Unknown author

My dad made no secret of the fact that he disliked his father. He also made no secret of how much he pitied his mother. There was no respect, only obligation. Anyone with a heart would wonder why he so willingly sent me off to stay with them so frequently when he knew his father was vile and his mother incapable of very much.

I don't know whether there was still fear there (my dad was a big man but, when you've been abused, it doesn't matter that you have grown up; you will always feel like a child around them), so he felt he had to send me. as a child, and even now, I wondered if he just didn't care enough about me, and he was just happy to get me out of the house.

Once I had disclosed my abuse, many years later, my mum, a couple of my aunties, and a couple of cousins, all said he had been inappropriate with them (again, why did those adults think I would be safe with him?!). I was his favourite, though. I got "special treatment".

Every time I got dropped off at their house, I would be told, "Look after your Nan." A frequent reminder that I was only alive to care for others.

My grandfather, unusually in those times, did all of the cooking. They would always be heavy Mediterranean meals. He would frequently buy me recipe books because he wanted me to share this love. Daytimes were usually spent in his kitchen, as he cooked for the week. I can still remember the smells: the delicious aromas of tomato-based pasta sauces were lovely. Some days, though, it would be the smells of boiling pig's trotters or some other poor animal's brains; the thought of those smells still turns my stomach. I wasn't allowed to leave the kitchen; I had to learn.

During the days, he would touch me frequently; most of the time, it was gentle, a show of grandfatherly affection, much like my other grandfather gave. Sometimes, it wasn't, and bits of my body would be grabbed and groped; I would get squashed against doors and walls (mostly in that bloody conservatory!) as he rubbed himself against me.

The days were horrible.

The nights were so much worse.

Other adults said it was because he was tight that he didn't turn the lights on when it got dark. There was some truth in that; he made Scrooge look generous. But, for me, I think he enjoyed the fear we felt. Neither my nan nor I liked sitting in the dark, and that was the way he liked it.

Both sets of grandparents lived on the same road; my parents knew each other most of their lives. With the exception of the conservatory, their houses were the same. How they were set out was very different.

In my maternal grandparents' house, the lounge was set up like most lounges: focused on the television but also so that everyone could chat. In my paternal grandparents' house, the lounge was set up like a tube train; the room was long and narrow; from the window at the front of the house to the doors to the conservatory, there were two sofas and an armchair; my uncle sat on the sofa closest to the window; he was a smoker so would often open the window to blow the smoke out; my grandfather's armchair was in the middle, much higher than the two sofas either side; my nan would sit tucked into the far end of the other sofa, closer to the TV; and, when I was there, I would sit next to her. I say sit; I would use my body as a shield, protecting her from him.

In the evenings, he would insist on watching scary programmes and films; this was the era of *Tales of the Unexpected, Hammer House of Horrors*, and late night horror films. My nan and I were scared of the programmes, but we were not allowed to turn away. Watching bloody tales of horror sat in the dark was spine-chilling. My nan and I would try not to respond to the horrors on the screen; he liked to hear us vocalise our fear.

It was horrible.

But it still wasn't the worst part.

Because of my "special-ness", I had my own bedroom; I had no say in how it was decorated or what was in there, or who, but it emphasised to everyone that I was his favourite.

Sometimes, I even got to stay in that room for the whole night. I would always start the night there.

You see, mostly, it was for show. Some nights, he did sleep in there with me, but most nights, I would be taken into his bed. Sometimes, my nan would be told to leave the bed and go to my room. Other times, she would just roll over and pretend to be asleep, while he did what he wanted to me.

He would tell me that what he was doing to me was the way to show someone how much you loved them. He would tell me that no one else loved me as much as he did, and that's why they weren't doing these things to me. He would tell me not to tell anyone, because they would be jealous he didn't love them as much, and then they would love me even less than they did already.

As a child who felt unloved and worthless, actually, just as a child, with an adult telling me these things, I believed him.

As with most survivors of childhood sexual abuse, I don't remember everything. It's an act of survival; you shut down to get through the horror. You shut down so that you are quiet because abusers often don't like noise. You shut down because being fully present is utterly soul destroying and terrifying.

Although I was a tall child, I was still only a child, and my grandfather was a big man. I remember him pinning me on my back. I remember pain. I remember his face above me. I can remember feeling suffocated by his breath. And then I remember darkness, like I disappeared — I stopped existing.

When I was around nine or ten, my mum gave me a book, *The Body Book* by Claire Raynor. It was a biology based book aimed at children, covering how our bodies work and how our bodies are made, including a section on sex. I sat and read it cover to cover. Afterwards I said to her,

"Did you know that bogeys are black before they get covered in green?"

She tutted at me.

"I gave you the book so you would learn about the stuff at the back!", she said disparagingly. The chapter about sex was near the end of the book.

I felt confused. I had read the book, as she had asked; and I had learned things from it, as she asked. And the stuff at the back of the book, well, I had been doing those things for quite some time by then, so I didn't need to learn more. But I couldn't say any of that to her. My grandfather had told me no one would want me around if I told them about "us" (he saw us as a unit), so I couldn't tell her about that.

But I always felt like I was never good enough for my mum, and I didn't want to disappoint her again.

There didn't seem to be a right answer, so I did what I spent most of my childhood and adolescence doing, and I went to my bedroom to be alone, thinking I couldn't do anything wrong there. I believed that if I stayed away from my family, I couldn't annoy them, or upset them, or disappoint them; if I was a good girl everywhere, then eventually, they might love me.

End of chapter note: How are you feeling? Are you okay? There are organisations detailed in the back of the book if you feel the need to talk to someone. Please know you are not alone; there is support if you need it.

Chapter Eight

Truth hurts

"The truth hurts, but silence kills." — *Mark Twain*

Many years later, when I was 21, I was visiting from London for a few days. My mum, my youngest sister, and I went to visit an auntie. We all sat around her dining table, chatting.

By this point. I had been living away from home for two years and I had been working continually. I was in a relationship; I was continuing to be the "good girl".

My middle sister was out clubbing at least once every weekend, getting drunk, meeting lots of men (I had no issue with her doing that, but I thought my parents might), and showing no signs of leaving home. During her teenage years, she spent a lot of time hanging around with friends in the local park, drinking and smoking. She didn't work as hard as I did at school; she didn't do as well academically.

I don't recall what started the conversation, but at one point, my mum turned to me with disgust and said:

"It doesn't matter what [sister] does; no child will ever be as difficult as [my birth name] was."

Initially, that statement made me feel upset; even though I had been a "good girl" by everyone else's standards, I still wasn't good enough for her.

But, by the time I had got back to the home I shared with my then partner, I was really angry! I had tried to do everything right and I still wasn't good enough!

And that's when I had my first breakdown.

All the years of feeling unloved and worthless. All the years of being regularly raped and keeping it a secret. All the years of trying to be who I thought my parents, and the rest of my family, might want. And I had failed. I would never be good enough.

I found a survivors' group that ran on a Thursday evening, and my partner and I would go along; I would be in the main room, with all the survivors, and he would be in the room for supporters of survivors. I needed to try to make sense of what had happened.

A few weeks later, he and I had plans to return to my home city to go to the theatre with my parents and sisters, to see *Buddy, The Musical* on the Saturday night.

I don't remember much about the show at all. I spent the whole time knowing I was going to disclose about the abuse when we got back, thinking they wouldn't believe me, thinking they were going to hate me more, thinking they may never want to see me again (a few people in the survivors' group had said this had happened to them with their families).

We got back to the house, and I sent my sisters to bed. I told them that, hopefully, I would explain tomorrow, but that I needed to talk to our parents first. They started guessing, assuming I was either pregnant or getting engaged.

My parents thought the same. Knowing that they would be really happy if they were going to have a grandchild, as they had told me that was what they expected, I felt the crushing doom of even more disappointment from them.

Jim, my boyfriend at the time, sat near me, looking really awkward; he had wanted to support me in telling them, but as big as he was, my dad was bigger and quite imposing, so he felt a different kind of fear.

With lots of deep breaths, I told them. I didn't tell them the gory details; I told them that my grandfather had abused me. For years.

They believed me. That was a relief!

They asked when it had started. I told them that it started soon after we moved back to the city.

They asked when it had stopped.

I told them the last time he had done anything was when he, my grandmother, and my uncle took me to his home country for a holiday, when I was 11. My dad made a comment about how he, my grandfather, always spoiled me. That hurt.

They asked why.

When I was away with them, in the Mediterranean country where he had spent his first couple of decades, towards the end of the holiday, I got sunstroke. My grandfather, with his darker skin, didn't believe he needed sun care; my grandmother in her constant need to be more acceptable to him, would use olive oil so she would get really tanned (basically frying herself), so they didn't use lotion on me.

We had a two bedroom apartment, and to keep up the pretence, I was sharing with my grandmother. We had single beds.

I've had sunstroke a few times, but that first time was the worst. I was being sick; I was dizzy; my head was pounding; and I was quite confused. Add to this the fact that my EB (epidermolysis bullosa), which was undiagnosed at that time, gets especially triggered by heat and friction, everywhere I was badly sunburnt had small blisters and my feet were covered in huge ones. A doctor came, but he didn't speak English, so I don't know what he said. As a child, no one thought it should be explained to me.

I was in bed for the last two or three days of the holiday. On the penultimate day, my grandfather came into our room; I could hear my grandmother approaching, then, when she heard him talk, I could hear her walk away. He said, as he fondled his penis, that I knew what I did to him and that, because I had been ill, I had deprived him of meeting his needs.

I could hear my grandmother approaching again, this time with louder, more deliberate footsteps, the familiar slapping of her flip flops. As he turned to ask what she wanted, I had a moment of clarity.

I knew how ill I had been, and he was telling me off that he couldn't do what he wanted to me. I knew in that moment that that wasn't love.

As he started to approach me again, I vomited. He left me alone.

The next day, my parents collected the four of us from the airport; these were the days before cars had to have seat belts in the back of the car, so my uncle sat in the front with my dad, and I, my mum, and my grandparents squeezed onto the back seat. He sat next to me and the entire journey home I tried to flatten myself close to my mum. I was repulsed by him and scared of him. Some of the fear came from concern that he would tell my parents how bad I had been. I had believed everything he said — if they found out, they would love me even less.

As I recounted this to my parents in their living room that Saturday night (missing out the bits about them hating me if they found out), I could see my dad getting angrier and my mum starting to cry.

After I finished telling them about why the abuse had stopped, my dad asked if there was anything else I wanted to say. I shook my head no.

He got up, left the room, then went and broke down the garden shed with his hands, throwing things in anger.

My mum went into the kitchen to wail.

Neither of them comforted me.

The next day, I told my sisters, separately. My middle sister, who, like my dad, rarely showed emotion, didn't really say anything; she listened, then she went to her room.

My youngest sister, who was 13, cried. She said that our uncle had started cornering her and touching her. Thankfully, with me disclosing, she was never left alone with them again. But, yes, we still had to see them. They were family, and family is important. Apparently.

We actually had a nice Sunday afternoon together before Jim and I headed back to our home.

For a brief moment, it felt like I mattered.

End of chapter note: How are you doing? I'm afraid the book is still hard going for a few more chapters yet, but I can promise you that it does get far happier in the second part.

Chapter Nine

Unloved

"Another reason it's dangerous to acknowledge that you were unloved is that it implies the possibility that your mother may have been right — you are unlovable." — Victoria Secund

On the Thursday after, I got a call from one of my sisters; she was crying, and I could hear my mum and other sister crying. My dad had decided to leave. He said it was my fault.

As I did so many times when there was family drama, I rushed back to my home city. I immediately went into protect and fix mode. I could feel the niggling pain inside of me. Of course it was my fault. Everything was always my fault. I shouldn't have said anything. I shouldn't have shared. It would have been kinder to keep it to myself.

I tried to ignore the quiet little voice saying, "But you'd have died if you hadn't shared. This needed to come out of you, so that you didn't continue to rot from the inside out."

What would it have mattered if I continued to rot? I meant nothing.

By the time I had got to the family home, my dad had already left, and my mum and sisters were distraught. I didn't cry. I couldn't cry; I had to support and fix. And I had to drive my mum to tell her siblings and parents. I didn't know that she was a narcissist then. But I knew she loved attention, so I shouldn't really have been surprised that she wanted an audience for her pain.

We drove to an auntie's house; many of the family were there. They all hovered as mum did her dying swan act at the top of the room:

"[He's] left me!"

There were gasps all round. My parents had previously been considered to be the perfect couple by observers. They always looked like a united front. They regularly demonstrated the affection they still had for each other (no child likes to see that!). They would tell people how happy they were. But I lived inside it. I remember saying to a friend when I was 11 or 12 that I wished my parents would divorce; I hated when mum shouted; I hated when dad ignored us; and I think I hoped that, if they weren't battling each other, there would be some spare love for me. I learned quickly that that wouldn't be true.

There were questions being asked; my mum sobbed, my sisters sniffled, and I stood, taking on all the guilt that this wouldn't be happening if it wasn't for me.

The family berated Dad; they brought up all their long held feelings of how they had always known he was unreliable; how they had always known he wasn't decent; how they had expected this to happen; she was far better off without him; he's not a good bloke like his dad. Oh! How that one hurt!!

After dramatically sobbing for a decent length of time, my mum answered one of the many whys coming at her.

"Because of her!" — as she pointed at me.

Cue! Scene! Curtains down! Interval.

Except this wasn't a play. This was my life. And every eye in the room was now focused on me.

I mumbled something about having to tell my parents something and that Dad hadn't reacted well to the news. No, I'm not pregnant. No, I'm not getting married.

Then an uncle (an uncle who was my dad's brother, married to my mum's sister, which is why he was there) said:

"He's never been good like dad. Dad stood by mum with all the shit she put him through. Dad will be so disappointed in him."

I never planned to tell the rest of the family, wanting to keep it just between us five; not feeling brave enough to answer the questions, take on the blame.

But, that statement was too much.

I tried to hold back my tears as I tried to raise my voice.

"My dad can be horrible, but he has never sexually abused me. Not like your dad!"

Silence. Just for a while.

No one looked surprised.

And my uncle shrugged his shoulders, dismissing me, and everyone carried on dealing with the wailing (not quite a) widow.

My experiences invalidated again. Yet more proof that I didn't matter.

I put my feelings back in their box and locked them away. I had to do the only thing I was good for and look after my family.

A few days later we found out that my dad had been having an affair with a woman for several years and he used me as his excuse to get out. If I hadn't said anything, he would still be here, I was told. They seemed to ignore the fact that he had been cheating; it was far better to have me to blame.

A few months later, Dad had found a flat to live in, my middle sister had moved in with him, and they were having a housewarming party. Jim and I were invited.

I felt really anxious, Jim felt really anxious, so we both tried to disappear into the cabinet as we munched on the tin of chocolates.

The woman he had left my mum for came over. She eyed me up and down. I may as well have been wearing a neon sign that said, "this is the BIG sister, and not just in age!!". In truth, I was a UK size 12 but the years of being told how fat I was had me believing I was massive.

She told me that I had probably better stop gorging on the chocolates because I didn't want to get any bigger. She was sickly sweet about it; a faux motherly caring.

In a rare act of bravery, I said:

"I don't drink. I don't smoke. And I don't fuck other women's husbands. I think I'm good with the chocolates, thanks."

She looked appalled and walked away. We left soon after. Oddly, we weren't invited back.

Over the next couple of years, my parents got back together and separated a further five times, with him going back to his mistress each time; they then didn't speak for 14 years; made contact (because of me); got married again; separated again. They were miserable together and miserable apart. Some would say it was a lifestyle choice.

With my parents separating that first time, everything became about that. Very soon after my announcement at the gathering, the whole family, aunts, uncles, cousins, knew what had happened to me. At least, they knew I had been abused but not to what extent.

Then Jim told his parents about my history.

End of chapter note: How are you feeling? Remember to look after yourself. Maybe take some deep breaths or have some chocolate or a cup of tea.

Chapter Ten

Without trust

"A relationship without trust is like a car without gas, you can stay in it all you want, but it won't go anywhere." – Unknown

His mum, a paediatric nurse, the font of all wisdom to Jim, told him that all abused people went on to abuse. She told him he should leave me because our children would never be safe around me.

He knew it wasn't true, but he idolised his mum. With those words in his head, and my mental health deteriorating, it was the beginning of the end. I believe he loved me. I also believe that, for a young man, for him, everything I was going through was too much. He couldn't understand the dynamics of a dysfunctional family, or the mental health of a crumbling lover, because he had never come across it before. We broke up.

But we sort of stayed together.

My wonderful employers at the time loaned me the money to go and visit a friend in Canada for Christmas. They knew Jim and I had broken up, they knew there were difficulties with my family (both of them were trained counsellors so they were great to be working for when I was struggling), and they knew I was missing a friend, who had returned to her family home, so they offered to loan me the money to go and see her.

Jim and I continued to meet. As friends. With benefits. We always ended up in bed, reassuring each other we weren't getting back together; it was just doing something we enjoyed.

He was concerned about me going to Canada alone; he knew I had wanted to move there straight from college, but my mum had convinced me not to (as I was continually seeking her approval, I agreed not to go), so he was worried I would stay. He was unhappy with me travelling all that way alone. He was anxious that I might meet someone. He wasn't sure whether he wanted me, but he was sure he didn't want anyone else to want me.

I had a wonderful time! I was immediately accepted into a loving family, and it was beautiful! My friend and her family took me to gorgeous places. We even climbed a mountain and made snow angels on Christmas Eve! On Christmas Day we went to visit their friends and neighbours: all of them had bought me gifts! It was so welcoming and kind! We spent time with her friends; we shopped; I even went on a date with two men on the same night! They were two friends: they both wanted to take me out, but I only had one night free, so we went out as a threesome. It was fantastic! I had so much fun!

I also realised how much my heart was hurting for Jim. I loved him; I missed him; I wanted him.

Within a couple of days of returning to the UK, Jim told me he felt the same, that me being away had made him realise how much I meant to him, how he didn't want to be that far from me ever again. We got back together. Within a few weeks we were engaged. Yes! We were going to spend our lives together!

A few weeks later, it was all over again. His mum had got to him. I was not marriage material. I was damaged goods. I would never make a good mother.

As with our last separation, we continued to see each other.

I was on the contraceptive pill, but one time, I had been ill, so we used a condom too.

I didn't see him for a few weeks, as we were both trying to move on; then I found out I was pregnant. The condom, on our last night together, must have split.

I didn't tell anyone for a while; I wanted to be sure. I needed to decide what I was going to do if Jim didn't want to be part of the baby's life. When I had decided that I would go ahead, irrespective of what he said, I told him. I phoned him. He got upset. He needed time to think about it. I said I would give him that time, but that I would like his support when he was ready.

I didn't hear from him. Days passed. Then a couple of weeks. A month. Longer.

Then, on a Sunday afternoon, alone in the little flat he and I shared, I started to have a miscarriage. The pain was horrific. The amount of blood was shocking. I spent the day either in the bathroom or curled up in a ball in the hallway, just outside the bathroom door.

I called Jim. He cried. He called his mum (he was living back at home with them); she told me that I was putting it on; that I was lying; I just wanted to trap her innocent boy. She hung up. I never saw any of them again.

My mum always called on a Sunday afternoon. I picked up the phone, hoping it would be Jim, saying he had been an idiot and was on his way. But it wasn't.

I told my mum what was happening; she got upset. Not about me. She wasn't bothered about my pain; she was upset that I hadn't told her about her first grandchild and now they were dead. What had I done to make this happen?!

The next day, I got up, cleaned the blood from the floors, and caught a bus to work. No one knew any different.

At the time, as devastated as I was, I consoled myself, telling myself that there would be more opportunities for me to have children; that the one I had lost wouldn't be forgotten but there would be others to follow. I didn't record the date (I didn't record dates of anything then). I went into a numb state where my body was there, going through the motions, but my mind had shut down. I was grieving, and I felt so lonely.

Unfortunately, there have been no more children. That was my one chance. Whether it's because of one of my conditions, or the damage a grown man did to an eight year old's body, or any of a number of other reasons, my body decided that having children was not going to be a feature in my life. Because of having mental health conditions, no matter how high functioning I am, the local social services refused to put me forward to adopt. I'm so grateful that I have had so many children in my life; I'm grateful to have seen so many school plays, carol concerts, day trips, holidays; but, as happy as I am with my life now, I shall always be grieving that I have never had my own.

There I was, grieving my lost baby, grieving a broken relationship, trying to deal with all the feelings associated with acknowledging abuse, feeling isolated and alone, and my parents had gone through another mammoth get together and break up, their last before their 14-year gap. So I had to be there for my mum.

She and my youngest sister would come to stay most weekends. It had nothing to do with me. They just wanted to get away from home, and I was somewhere free to sleep and be fed.

We all wallowed. A lot. And there were arguments. My mum would say that my loss was nothing like hers; that hers was more real, more powerful. Mine was nothing. Jim and I had only been together two years! What did I know about loss?!

And she liked to threaten suicide. It was horrible. So many times she would say that her life wasn't worth living. That, if it wasn't for [youngest sister] she would end it all. Nobody else mattered, just my little sister.

One day, after many, many of her reminders that my losses were nothing, that I was not worth staying alive for, I got angry. I told her that she had every opportunity to kill herself, that she could even do it on the drive home; I told her that she either do it or stop trying to make me feel bad for existing and never mention it again. I felt hugely guilty and regretted saying it immediately.

But she never mentioned suicide again. She did, however, continue to make me feel bad for existing.

End of chapter note: A gentle reminder that there are organisations listed at the back of the book if you feel the need to talk to anyone. Be kind to yourself, please.

Chapter Eleven

Above her station

"But, were it not for frustration and humiliation I suppose the human race would get ideas above its station." — *Ogden Nash*

My mum started dating other men. A couple of them came to stay when she came up. I never felt comfortable having these strange men in my home, but she told me I had to accept them. The threat was always there that if I didn't accept them, I would lose her; I still craved to be accepted by her, so I gave in every time.

Alongside all of this, my beloved maternal grandfather had finally retired, well into his 70s. He got ill soon into his retirement. Logically, it was probably because 60 years of work had caught up with him, or that the reason behind his retirement was that his body was struggling. To my family, it was something else to blame me for. If I hadn't disclosed about the abuse, he wouldn't have started worrying about it, and he wouldn't be ill. It was my fault. He was adored by all of us, and there I was, killing him.

That's fine; let's just heap that guilt on top of everything else I was living with.

One time, he and my nan, and my mum and little sister, came to visit me in my tiny flat — the flat I had shared with Jim, before he moved out. I was telling them that I had found a new job; I was returning to being a live-in nanny, and I was going to start studying again. The course was specifically for people who wanted to apply to university as mature students, and I planned to then apply to do teacher training. He was elated! He told me I was going to change the world! That children everywhere needed me! His belief in me was so wonderful!

When I was at school, my careers teacher always said I should be a teacher; I didn't feel I was clever enough, so I focused on childcare options: parentcraft (a curriculum option in the 1980s), home economics, sewing.

I applied to college to do a childcare course. When I went for the interview, the two teachers kept telling me that I was too clever to work in childcare and that I should do A Levels instead — I have always found that statement really troubling; wouldn't people want intelligent people looking after their children? It was indicative of how poorly valued all care workers are. Nevertheless, I still didn't believe I was clever enough, but as I already had maths and English qualifications and didn't need to repeat them with all the other girls on the course, I agreed that I would add one A Level.

Those two teachers, a few months into the two year course, encouraged me to do all my coursework in one year (I already had plenty of childcare experience so that was covered) and do another A Level and some GCSEs. I was the first, and youngest, person to ever do that course in one year. And I passed with the highest level possible.

Obviously, I went home, proudly clutching my results, expecting that this would be the time my family would be proud of me! This would be when they finally accepted me!

Of course it wasn't.

My dad asked if this would mean I would now get a proper job like [middle sister]. She was doing a Youth Training Scheme, earning £25 a week, working five days; I was full time at college and working a few hours at the weekend at a local newsagent, earning exactly the same amount (except I earned more at the shop and doing childcare during the college holidays). I still wasn't good enough.

During my second year at college, I applied to universities to do teacher training. I got accepted at all five of the ones I applied to. My parents refused to pay for me to go. Back then, funding was much better, so they wouldn't have had to pay so much, but, no, I wasn't allowed to go to university. I was told I had "ideas above my station."

Which was why, six years later, I was telling my grandparents that I was planning to go, as a mature student. My nan, stoic as ever, wasn't effusive, but he, my grandfather, was so proud. They didn't know that I had been told I couldn't go years before. I was the first woman in the family who would be going to university, and he was delighted!

Two years later, I had completed the Access Course, moved to the West Country to live with Tom, been accepted on to a degree course to study psychology (not teaching), and my gorgeous grandfather died two weeks before I started. His funeral was the day before my first day.

End of chapter note: Cup of tea time? A rest? Please look after you.

Chapter Twelve

Thoughts aren't facts

"It is the mark of an educated mind to be able to entertain a thought without accepting it." — Aristotle

My first day at university, I felt lonely, scared, and completely out of my depth. How the hell did I get there?!!

I loved university, but I constantly felt like I was a fraud. I'll talk about Tom's impact on my time at university elsewhere in this book. With him telling me I was nothing without him, and with a lifetime of my family telling me conflicting messages about my intelligence (you're too smart for your own good/you're not as clever as you think you are/you're so stupid), I doubted I could study at university level.

I also doubted I would make any friends; I was basing my limited knowledge on friends at university on films set on American campuses (lots of drinking and sex; I was pretty much teetotal and in a monogamous relationship), or on films set in Oxbridge (lots of highly intellectual conversations, drinking and sex; I didn't feel bright enough for those and see previous comment).

It didn't cross my mind that there was probably a high percentage of other people who were possibly feeling the same as me, maybe not for the same reasons but still valid fears, nonetheless.

I did make friends, just a few, and I loved them. And, academically, I did okay. I was very rarely at the top of the class, but neither was I often at the bottom; I was very much average.

Those friends probably thought I was quite confident. I have always been great at covering my true thoughts; it's a survivor's tool. In truth, I was scared and confused, baffled as to how I was going to get through.

We had to do experiments in our health sciences classes; I always let others lead the way. I remember the first experiment, which had little to do with the course itself but was more a test to see if we understood how to use lab equipment.

We had to see if woodlice like dark, damp conditions, or dry, light ones (challenging, eh?). I put a wet piece of that blue paper towel stuff on one side of the petri dish and sellotaped it down, then placed a few woodlice in the centre; as one intrepid woodlouse made its way to its chosen destination, one of its legs got stuck on a piece of Sellotape that had curled up! It lost a leg! I had to hold back tears! I was devastated; I felt so cruel. Due to my idiocy, the fact I wasn't even smart enough to stick down Sellotape correctly. I had injured a poor little creature. Add that to an incident a few years previously where I had accidentally stepped on a woodlouse and killed it in my haste to get away from a large spider, I have HUGE guilt about woodlice, and I STILL apologise when I see one. When you are brought up being told everything is your fault, guilt comes too easily and you end up feeling responsible for things many, many years longer than is necessary. This perceived ineptitude meant I didn't trust myself to do anything in the lab without support.

We were told early on that we would be expected to give presentations. From the second I heard that, I was dreading them. I couldn't even cope with people looking at me while they sang me "Happy Birthday", and I certainly didn't think I had anything of any interest to say. How on earth was I going to pass any module that specified I had to do this?!

The first presentation was approaching. We were each given a subject to discuss. Mine was Freud's interpretation of the

Powerful Penis and the Vulgar Vagina. I already knew I disliked Freud intensely, which didn't help. I prepared everything.

In those days (the deep, dark days of yore: the 1990s), we used overhead projectors. I had my transparency sheets ready; I had written out everything I was planning to say; and, apart from actually practising the presentation, as I was relying on my usual behaviour patterns of if I fail because I didn't try hard enough, that's more bearable than if I fail because I'm stupid; I had everything ready.

Firstly, I kept putting the transparencies on back to front or upside down or both. This was going well!

Then the talking started. I hadn't realised before this incident that, although I knew I used my hands to express myself when I talked, I didn't know that my hands become incredibly expressive with my increased nerves. With each mention of Freud's powerful penis, my left arm would rise; with every mention of the vulgar vagina, my hands would flap. As the audience laughed, I got more anxious. As I got more anxious, my voice became raised on the keywords in the presentation and my hand movements got bigger. Soon, my left arm was thrusting into the air with every POWERFUL PENIS and my arms were flapping as if I was trying to tread water in an incredibly rough vertical sea every time I practically shouted VULGAR VAGINA. Everyone was crying with laughter. Everyone but me. I was mortified. I had obviously failed in such a spectacular fashion that my only option was to leave the university and move to a remote nunnery in the Himalayas.

However, in the feedback, the lecturer told me that I had given all of the important points in a very amusing way (she thought it was deliberate!), and that she had never laughed so much, so she gave me a high mark. Now, when I'm preparing to do some public speaking, I always tell myself that it will never be that bad, and that came with good results, which I find reassuring.

On my first day of university, I remember a student walking into the room; I loved her look and I said to myself that, with her individual style and the way she moved, I wanted to look like her, be as confident as her, and, most of all, I wanted to be deemed worthy enough to be her friend. A few weeks later, we were paired together, and we hit it off. We became really close friends really quickly. Apparently, she had had similar thoughts about me when she saw me; it's interesting how much we can hide behind masks.

She, Kate, was the first friend I felt safe telling almost everything to; I loved her so much. We didn't always study the same modules, but we shared so much of the experience. I would spend time around at the house she shared with her partner, and she would spend time at the house I shared with Tom (not often when he was there, though).

When Tom and I had a temporary separation, Kate offered me their spare room, where I stayed for a week.

Kate had agoraphobia and a fear of the dentist; over the years, I got her to make dental appointments that I accompanied her to, and we had adventures in places she had previously felt too anxious to go to; we even had a few days in a European capital together!

Throughout the break, we did everything at her pace; we only tried things she felt able to do. I have a fear of flying but, as with most things, if someone needs my support, I can hide my concerns to help them through theirs.

The flight out was fine but, soon after getting on the return flight, I knew there was a problem with the plane. The air stewards were whispering to each other as they looked furtively around; things that we had watched be brought onto the plane were being moved off. Then we were all told that there was a problem and that we were changing planes. I felt anxious but glad we were moving. We got on one of those airport buses and drove around until we got to the new plane.

Kate made a joke about it being the same plane; until then I had been a little fidgety but hadn't expressed my concerns. At her joke, I panicked. When we landed and we were on our way back home, she told me she was grateful that I faked a panic attack to reassure her that I had issues too, so that she didn't feel guilty at how much of our holiday was focused on her needs. She didn't believe it was real because she never saw me like that.

Our friendship continued after we had both left university (her a year before me as I had to take a year out). She stayed in the city we studied in, and I moved to London, and then back to my birth city. I thought she was the best friend I had ever had.

Then, my mental health started struggling. As I have mentioned elsewhere in the book, being near my family again had brought up a lot of stuff I had been running from; the monsters that live under our beds had come out and were talking to me all the time.

I was very aware of Kate's fragile mental health, so I always ensured I checked on her regularly. And I thought I was playing down my issues.

Then she stopped returning my calls and texts. I was incredibly concerned; I thought something awful had happened. I was worried she was really unwell; I questioned whether her partner would tell me if there was a problem. So, I wrote her a letter. I told her I was worried about her because I hadn't heard from her. I told her that there was nothing I wasn't willing to help her with. I told her that, if I didn't hear from her, even if all it was only a text to say, "I'm okay", by the following Friday, I was going to get the train there and knock on her door until I saw she was okay.

A few days later, I got a postcard. All it said was:

[Birth name], Your friendship repels me. Kate

My heart broke. I loved her so much and yet, here she was, saying how little I meant to her.

I don't think any non-familial relationship ending hurt me as much as this one. With the relationships with men, I never gave myself fully; I had been taught that no one would love me if they really knew me, and I really wanted those men to love me, so I tried to be the girlfriend they wanted. They saw some of my vulnerabilities, but even with Jim, who was with me during my first breakdown, I kept a lot back from him.

With Kate, we seemed to share so much that I trusted her more than I had ever trusted another human. With the men, I could justify it; I could tell myself that they didn't really know me. I could tell myself that I had never fully trusted them, so I kept large parts of myself hidden. I could tell myself that they weren't really interested in the real me, just the parts of me they wanted. I could justify why they all ended. With Kate, the first person to know more of me than anyone else had ever known, this felt like a huge rejection and a huge failure on my part.

How on earth could I have thought that anyone would really like me if they knew the true me? Why, in my tiny, stupid mind, did I think that someone would think I was valuable as a whole being? Yup, I was truly heartbroken. Yet again, I had been told that my feelings, my needs, weren't worthy of compassion. Yet again, I was being told that my only value was in supporting others and that it was despicable of me to say I needed help.

Over the years, I have learned time and again that some people can only be in relationships where they are the one getting support. They know how to be the person accepting help, but they don't know how to give it. Equally, there are people who only know how to give it and struggle with accepting it. I know; I've been that person for a large part of my life.

I truly believe that Kate just didn't know how to be adaptive; she didn't know how to support me because I had appeared to "bounce back" after everything she'd seen me go through (I didn't bounce back; I just felt I couldn't need support for too long because no one would stay around if I did); and rather than admit she didn't know how to do something, she turned on me. I still miss the friendship I thought we had.

End of chapter note: How are you feeling? If my story is bringing up emotions for you, perhaps you could write them down? It might help if they're difficult emotions, and it will be good to read back if they're positive ones.

Chapter Thirteen

It doesn't define me

"Trauma may happen to you, but it can never define you." —
Melinda Longtin

It's interesting. I hadn't considered myself a victim of domestic abuse. I had said I lived with an abusive partner, but, for some reason, it didn't click that I had lived in a domestic abuse situation. That changed when I went on a course to learn more about domestic abuse. I thought it would be useful in my work, and, as the training meant I would become a Champion for their organisation, meaning that, on seeing my badge, people would either talk to me and learn more, or know that I am a safe person to talk to, I thought it was a good thing to do all round.

At first, when they mentioned there would be quizzes, I got anxious. I thought the other people in the session were far more experienced than me and that I would look like an idiot when I showed I knew very little.

Then the first quiz started, all multiple choice questions. I wrote my answers. All right!! Oooooh! I thought. I know more than I think I do.

Then the information started coming.

As I wrote each characteristic of what constitutes a domestic abuse relationship, memories came flooding back.

I was with Tom for almost four years. We met the day after my 24th birthday in a pub in southwest London; he was there with a friend of mine. He and I got on immediately; after a long while of spending time in pubs with men who seemed constantly drunk (it was a rugby area and we tended to go out after matches, so they were usually celebrating or commiserating), Tom impressed me with his intelligence and eloquence. At the time, I was studying on an Access Course, and one of the modules was philosophy. We were talking about this, and he said, "Yes, I've read Sartre in the original French." I was dazzled with his knowledge and his experience, and, as someone who had always doubted their intelligence, I was flattered that he wanted to talk to me.

As an aside, many years later, I read Sartre; if I had read it before I met Tom, I would possibly have been warned away (I did not like Sartre!).

He returned to his home in a West Country village and, over the next nine weeks, we talked every night on the phone, and we visited each other every weekend. I had started a new nanny job that I wasn't happy in (very rude family, with very strict guidelines), and as I was still in the trial period, I decided to leave; Tom suggested I move in with him and his parents. So, nine weeks after meeting him, I left London and moved to a tiny little village in the West Country.

It sounded idyllic. He and his parents lived in a chocolate box cottage surrounded by the beautiful Cotswolds. I had always thought, living mostly in cities, that I was really a country girl at heart and that this little village was going to be my spiritual home. It wasn't. I'm a city girl. From living on flight paths, busy roads, and all the noises of a city, I couldn't cope with the silence. Two fields over was a boarding kennel; in the early hours of every morning, the dogs would start barking and howling, upsetting me deeply. I wanted to traipse across the fields and keep them company. It got to the stage where, after not drinking alcohol for years, I began to have a glass or two of gin every night to get to sleep.

Tom and I met in November; we were engaged by February. He sat me down, told me what he was worth, told me how much better my life would be with him and his wealth, then said we would get married. He told me no one would love me as much as he did. Although I had lived through those lies before, as a child, I believed him. I needed to believe him. I needed to believe that someone could love me.

As an aside, I met Eddie Reader, lead singer of Fairground Attraction, a favourite band in the 80s, in 2019. I told her that, as a teenager, I would listen to her song, "Find My Love", and dream that that love would come to me. I didn't have it at home, so I longed to be loved by a family, to be part of a family. The song was never really about that "one true love" for me.

With Tom, I felt that I had found my love. His mum was wonderful, and his sister was the adult version of that cool kid at school everyone wants to be friends with. They accepted me. They included me. And Tom was always telling me how much he loved me.

Tom would go off to work every day, and I would be left at home; I didn't want to get in the way of his parents, so I hid in our bedroom most of the time. I knew no one else in the area to go out with, and I felt lonely. The closest bus stop was almost a mile away; it only ran once an hour (a bugger if you missed it!) and the last bus back was 5.30pm.

Tom wasn't bothered by my loneliness. He would tell me I had him and his friends; what more could I need? The naive me felt welcomed by that.

Tom had a desire to be a Charles Atlas type figure; sadly, for him, he was only ever going to be the before picture. He was a naturally slim man. He insisted I body build with him. He would tell me it was a bonding experience, something for us to share. He would tell me he knew how he could make my body the muscular body I wanted. The thing is, I don't recall ever saying I wanted to have a muscular body. But being the good girlfriend he insisted I needed to be, I would go to the gym with him, and I would train at home with him. I did get to be quite muscular.

He managed my food intake. Before he left for work, he would make me up a protein shake to have for breakfast. He would tell me what I needed to eat for lunch, and at 3pm every day, he would phone me to check that I was eating the large portion of chicken wings he said I had to eat. Protein! Protein! Protein! Monday to Friday, it was all about the gym and building muscle. I would be much more attractive if I was more muscular, he would tell me.

Then, Friday evening would come. He would always come home with a kilo bar of Dairy Milk or Galaxy. It seemed romantic; how lovely that my partner wanted to buy me gifts so frequently. And I do love chocolate!

But, I had to eat it. Not eat it over several days, but eat it that night, in front of him. He would get excited watching me gorge on these giant bars of chocolate. It didn't matter that I felt ill; don't I want to turn him on, he would ask. And I would be so much more attractive if I was fatter, he would say.

Definitely mixed messages there. But I didn't understand. I thought I must be stupid because I couldn't grasp what he was trying to do. He often told me that because I was a "bit mad" that I wasn't up to understanding. He would tell me that he loved me, that he wanted the best for me, and didn't I want to make him happy? He was so good to me; surely he deserved that I make him happy?

I did get more muscular and fatter. Rapidly, I went from a UK size 12 to a UK size 22. The body I had rarely felt at home in now felt like I was squatting in someone else's.

As I was only working part time at this point, he bought me clothes. He picked my clothes. Once I started university and not so wisely bought some clothes for myself with my grant money, the styles were very different. The clothes he bought me showed off my body, the body he claimed as his, with low necklines, high hemlines. The clothes I bought for myself hid me; I wasn't happy in my skin, and I felt I didn't deserve to be seen.

The university I went to wasn't one I intended to apply to, but he convinced me it was fantastic. He had gone there, and he had friends there. So, despite, surprisingly(!), being offered places at universities around the country, I went to his in Bristol. I didn't get a place there at first. He insisted I ring them and demand to know why; they told me why (lots of applicants) and offered me a place.

Although it wasn't my choice to go there, I loved the university I went to. As a mature student, at all of soon to be 25, I felt old, even though there were a few others who were older than me. I felt fat and frumpy. I felt like a fraud. The logic is I had good exam results from schools, and I had good results and recommendations from my Access Course. That wasn't in my head, though. In my head, I worried every day that someone was going to realise that I didn't deserve to be there, that I was stupid, that it was just luck that I got good results; it was just people being nice when marking my work because they felt sorry for pathetic me.

I anxiously waited to be found out. I waited to be made an example of in packed rooms, thinking a lecturer was going to bring me to the front of the room to humiliate me, to make an example of me, to the 100+ other people who really deserved to be there, to rebuke me for allowing my fat, ugly, stupid body, to take up the space of someone I had stolen a space from. That never happened, but still, I waited.

I made a few good friends at university. Despite all my concerns, I loved studying, and I loved the content. Well, most of it. I don't recall ever enjoying one second of statistics! Although Tom had wanted me to go to university, he didn't want it to affect his life, unless it was going to student events with his friend in the year above me. My friends were only included if they participated in the things he wanted to do. I wasn't allowed to study when he was at home; after all, he told me, he provided us with a nice house to live in, he allowed me to go to university, surely the least I could do was be fully present when he was home. It seemed a fair compromise at the time.

My friends at university knew nothing about my home life, not the truth of it. I told them how loving and attentive he was. I told them I loved to go to the gym with him (I loved that my nickname to university friends was Xena Warrior Princess because it felt like I had achieved something). I don't know whether any of them had thoughts about the realities of it. Did they ever wonder about his "attentiveness"? Did they ever ponder over why I rarely saw them socially?

I failed my second year of university; just the one module but they suggested I take most of the year out and only work on that one module, before returning to do my third year. The failure confirmed my suspicions. I was stupid, and I didn't deserve to be there.

At this point, the world was in the run up to Y2K, and as Tom was an IT specialist, he decided we would move to London, to live in his parents' apartment, so that he could be part of the huge amount of money that was being paid to people who could stop the predicted crash as a new millennium dawned. I returned to nanny work.

Things got worse.

He had always been reluctant to spend money (one friend relished saying he was "as tight as a gnat's chuff"). Apart from on our birthdays, he would nearly always start a row before we were due to go out for dinner or to the cinema alone; that way, we ended up staying at home and he didn't have to pay out anything. Even when I said I would pay, he would find reasons to not go, frequently telling me how wasteful I was. If we did go out, it was nearly always with his friends; that way, the bill could be split more ways. Even holidays, with the exception of one where we stayed in his dad's apartment in Spain, we went with his friends. I don't mean we went, they had their room, we had ours; we shared rooms, because that meant it was cheaper. He still insisted on sex, telling me to be quiet, covering my mouth.

He was, by nature, a night owl; he would happily stay up until almost dawn and sleep away the days. On many of those nights, I would go to bed and, just as I was drifting off, he would come into the bedroom and wake me up. It would either be because he was annoyed with me or because he wanted sex. At first, I hoped he would listen to me saying I was tired. He was always very apologetic about waking me up. Then, as I was almost asleep again, he would come in, wake me up again, try to be a bit more persuasive. If it was sex he wanted, he would offer to do things he told me he didn't usually like (he had no interest in my pleasure); if he was angry with me, he would get louder each time he came in. This would go on for hours.

There was one time that he insisted on inviting one of his friends and his girlfriend round. He wanted me to cook a fancy three course meal; he wanted me to impress them (his friend was also part of the Y2K boom, and they were constantly competing over who earned more and who was "better at money"). Tom had stayed up until dawn the night before, so it was me who cleaned the apartment, did the shopping, and prepared the meal. An hour before the friend and his girlfriend arrived, he got out of bed, showered, dressed, and made himself beans on toast. I served the dinner. He refused to eat any of it because why would he eat such crap? The friends told me it was a delicious meal; with each of their compliments, he would tell me they were lying. Cooking was something else I was useless at; he should have just made everyone beans on toast, because at least they would have enjoyed that.

To the outside world, I played the doting girlfriend. My family would visit for the odd day, and Tom would love to show off the beautiful apartment, the views, and we'd walk along the river to the lovely surprisingly country-like pub near the centre of London. It did do really good food, so that was often a place we visited whenever his friends or our families visited.

The last time we went there together was mortifying. I have a small bladder (not medically checked, just what goes in comes out fairly soon after), and as he was buying pints of Coke (cheaper than halves), I was needing to wee frequently. Before we left, I said I needed a wee, and he said we would be home soon, and I could wait. He didn't raise his voice; he didn't need to. He decided we would walk the long way home; not the beautiful scenic route but the way past a brewery, that he insisted he and his friend stand and admire for a long time, and through the estates, so he could show off that we were living in a posh area. He at least tripled the amount of time it would normally take to get home.

As we arrived on our estate, I increased my walking pace, desperate to get home. He kept up, muttering how pathetic I was that I was rushing, that I was behaving like a child; I couldn't even stand still to wait for the lift, so I ran up the two flights of stairs, him close behind. I ran into the bathroom and didn't even shut the door (I am NOT a communal toileting person, apart from with my cats; they use their tray frequently when I am in the bathroom). I started to pull my dress up and my pants down, but I was too late; he stood there as I wet myself and I cried; he kept tutting, saying how pathetic I was. When I had finished, he walked away, muttering about my pitiful being and shaking his head. I locked the door, cleaned up, and waited for his friends to come into the apartment and move into the lounge. I could hear him telling them what had happened. I could hear him laughing about it, about me. I ran from the bathroom, and I hid. I became a scared child, and I hid in a wardrobe, rocking back and forth, stifling my cries. I was utterly embarrassed and ashamed. When it was time for them to go, the female friend came in, found me, gently touched my arm, and said she would see me soon; there was pity and tenderness in her eyes. For the first time, I felt someone had seen what he was capable of.

He had no issues with embarrassing me in front of his friends, no concerns about my feelings. One time, he had invited several of his friends from his village to come and stay for the weekend. They arrived Saturday afternoon and the drinking started. I kept them topped up, I fed them, but I mostly stayed out of their way.

Then the porn went on. I could hear them all talking about the women in the films, about what they would do to them. Then Tom called me in.

He told me to stand where all his friends could see me. He then told his friends to say what they would like to do to me. They all looked almost as awkward as I felt. Their eyes lowered. So he decided he would start the ball rolling; he would tell them what he did to me. Most of it was lies, but I felt like he was showcasing me as the depraved whore he had previously called me. When his (very limited) imagination had run out of things to say, he told me to get out of the way so they could watch the porn stars and see that there were some women who really knew how to please their man.

Afterwards he justified all this as him thinking I was so beautiful that he wanted to brag to his friends that I was his. I felt no love, no romance in that statement; I was owned in the way a farmer owns a prized cow.

Despite all of this, and more, it was something quite small in comparison that tipped the balance. I had felt he was my last hope at being married, having a family, doing things the way that was expected, so I carried on, believing I deserved the treatment, believing I wouldn't get any better.

We had gone back to his family's for the weekend, and as always when we visited, on the Saturday night, we met up with his friends, then went for a curry and to their favourite nightclub, an Indie/Metal club. I'm not a huge fan of heavy metal music but the Indie stuff was good, so I danced to the stuff I liked, and, thankfully, because he was usually too drunk to notice, especially as he and all his friends were moshing, I could sit out the stuff I didn't like.

A young woman joined in with their circle. Every one of his friends there had a girlfriend, and even in their drunken states, they did not return her gaze, knowing all of us girlfriends were nearby. Tom didn't care. I watched as he flirted, touching her.

I walked to the bar, angry, and ordered another soft drink; he came up to me; he knew I was pissed off. He put his hand on my waist, told me he was just having some fun; he told me it didn't mean anything. I told him it meant something to me. He snatched his hand away and started telling me how unreasonable I was, how I was a killjoy, and he went back to the dance floor and continued his mating ritual.

That was when I realised that, even if I was single and alone for the rest of my life, I didn't want to spend another minute with him.

I took the car keys and drove back to his parents'. He woke me up, several hours later, throwing stones at the window; I let him in, and as soon as we were in the bedroom, he shouted. For the first time, I didn't respond. I just took it. I had found some resolve in myself, and I knew I had made the right decision.

I also knew that I had no money to leave him.

The next day, I drove us back to London and we barely spoke. Within a couple of days, things were back to his normal, but I had begun plotting.

I started adding extra things to our grocery shop, toothpaste, toothbrushes, toilet rolls, period products, and started to store them, ready for when I moved out. I started to look for work back in Bristol, ready for my final year at university, and I found a job as a live-in nanny that I could do around my studies. I didn't tell him.

For several months, I went through the motions. Of everything.

Every Sunday night, for months before and after the clubbing event, he would give me his signal, telling me he was ready for sex. I then had to go into our bathroom, smother myself with KY Jelly and then lie on the bed, legs apart, waiting for him to come in and penetrate me. It was always about his pleasure. I was just a warm, moist place to poke. When he had finished, I would get up, go into the shower, and scrub myself raw; scrubbing away his smell, his touch, and trying, but failing, to scrub away how disgusting I felt. He never noticed because he always fell asleep straight after.

Scrubbing myself raw was a coping mechanism. I had started self-harming when I was a child, around 6 or 7 years old. It started with burning myself as I made cups of tea for my parents. Maybe the first time it happened accidentally, and I enjoyed that I got rare attention, so I repeated the behaviour, but, after the first couple of times, I started getting told off, told I was clumsy. I carried on doing it, though, because, although I didn't get the attention and affection that every human needs, for a few moments all of my focus was on my physical pain, and not on my sadness and loneliness.

Once the sexual abuse started, that's when I started to have really hot baths and rub my skin with a loofah. I felt that people could see what others had said and done to me written all over my skin, and I desperately wanted to remove it all. I did use other methods of self-harm occasionally but burning was the "friend" I turned to most often.

Apart from the sadness that I felt to do this, what was also very sad was that people would sometimes compliment me on my very soft skin. In my wonky, desperate for approval, brain, that was like a reward; by damaging myself, I was doing something right.

Tom didn't really notice how distant I had become; I was still doing everything he asked of me, and he wasn't particularly perceptive. And we never talked about me leaving. I think he might have known, but he didn't want to admit it was happening.

It's odd how I wanted to soften the blow for him. The years I had spent with him in which my feelings weren't considered, yet when it came to me hurting him, I had to do it gently.

In the last weeks, as I was packing up to move, I told him that as he was still doing so well in London, it made sense for me to move back to Bristol and for him to stay in the apartment. The wonderful family, my favourite family, I was working for had asked me to stay working for them and had arranged to change their hours to two longer days, so I said to Tom that I would still be with him two nights a week. That placated him.

On the day of the move, he helped me load up the van I had hired, and we said an awkward goodbye. I told him I would be back the following week.

And I was. But I slept in the spare room. He never commented on it; I don't know why. Maybe he thought that he would be supportive. Maybe he wanted a break himself. I don't know, but I don't think so. Some of the time we actually had a lovely time. We would chat, and I was reminded why I fell in love with him; we would go to the cinema; we got on really well.

Most of the time.

Sometimes, he would return to his previous behaviours. I would be drifting off to sleep, and he would come in and wake me up. At first it would be him asking what had gone wrong with us; I would say it wasn't the time to talk about it. He would leave the room. Then he would come in and start offering sex acts. I would refuse; he would leave; then he'd come back, again as I was drifting off to sleep, and offer something else. The next days at work were harder, as I was so tired. I was working in London, working in Bristol, and doing a full time degree, so I was already tired; being woken up several times a night really did not help.

After a few months, I had to stop the commute and focus on my final few months of university. Tom and I stayed in touch; it always felt awkward, like he was trying too hard to be who he thought I wanted. He became more attentive, and he would offer bizarre things, like offering to let me drive his shiny new sports car. He was very possessive of his car so it was odd that he offered, especially as I am not someone who would be enamoured by a sports car.

A few months after university, my favourite family tempted me back to London by offering me a lovely flat as part of the deal. It was part time and they had arranged for me to meet another family who also wanted part time. I arranged to stay with Tom for the weekend of the interview. There was a club night happening that I regularly attended, since he and I had broken up, and I had friends who went. I thought Tom would be much more willing to let me stay if I invited him out with my friends; he had wanted to go to the club for a while.

One friend, Nicky, knew about his attempts to get me back, though not to the extent that she knew about everything — no one knew about that — and I asked her to be a bit of a bodyguard if he started getting a bit handsy with me once he started drinking. She agreed.

He did start getting handsy with me and, true to her word, she stepped in to stop him touching me. She did this by putting his hands on her and sticking her tongue down his throat. I felt that was a little too dedicated to the role but felt more relieved that he was distracted. I started to relax about spending the night at the apartment with him, feeling that, as he was obviously highly entertained by Nicky, he wouldn't do his usual.

I was wrong. Very wrong.

He didn't even wait until we got back.

He got into the back seat of the cab first and sat in the middle of the seat. I asked him to move over; he giggled and refused. I climbed in, put on my seat belt, and he moved even closer to me. He started to touch my leg; I removed his hand and reminded him that he had spent most of the night playing tonsil hockey with Nicky, trying to get him to focus on her again (that does sound mean, but I genuinely believed that he wouldn't treat her the way he did me). He kept saying, "but she's not you!" as he tried to get ever closer, touching my face, my hair, my arms, my legs.

When we got back to the apartment, I helped him up the stairs, sat him in the lounge, and offered to make him a drink before I went to bed. He said he was just going to sit for a bit.

I went into the spare room, closing the door, as always, and went to sit on the bed. The room had a double bed in the centre and a single bed tucked up against the wall; I always slept in the single bed. I was concerned that, by sleeping in the double, he would see that as an invitation to join me. I put my head in my hands and sighed. It felt like nothing I did would turn him away.

The bedroom door opened; as he approached, I stood up. It felt safer to stand than to be sitting on a bed. He had tears in his eyes.

He grabbed me to hug me. I tentatively returned the hug.

"Why have you hurt me so much?!", he wailed.

As well as being utterly baffled by the question, I was very aware of his tears and his snot being wiped on my neck and clothes.

I had no words. I felt I had deserved how he had treated me, after all, I had been told I was worthless and unlovable so many times, to have someone who professed love felt good, even if it didn't look how love in films and books looks. But I couldn't comprehend that I had hurt him. I really thought he would be glad to get rid of me.

"We are so good together! Why are you making it stop?!"

I whispered a scared, "But it wasn't all good."

He couldn't hear me over his sobs.

I calmed him down, walked him to the door, wished him good night, and then shut it.

I returned to the far side of the room, sat on the edge of the double bed, and started to unlace my boots.

Tom came back.

He sat next to me on the bed.

He moved closer so we were touching.

I moved away a little, closer to the end of the bed.

He moved closer. I moved away.

He moved closer. I moved away. I fell off the end of the bed.

Before I could even begin to sit back up, he was on top of me, pinning me down.

I, understandably, started to panic. My breathing became heavy and laboured. I was crying.

He kept saying how good we were together. Saying how much he loved me. All the time trying to kiss me as my head thrashed side to side.

He started to move his legs so that they were no longer pinning mine down, but instead he was using them to prise my legs apart.

I don't know where it came from, although I am ever so glad it came from somewhere, but I pushed him off me at the same time as using my right knee to jab him. Something in that action made him stop.

He sat up. He told me he loved me. He told me I had made him want to do that. Then he got up and left the room.

I sat and sobbed. Then I got ready for bed. I desperately needed to sleep. I had an interview the next morning and I had to be up at 8; it was already approaching 4am.

I thought he might have learned a lesson, so I thought I was safe to sleep.

Again, I was wrong.

He did his usual trick. He waited until I started to drift off and then he would come in. The first couple of times were to apologise. Then he started to offer sex acts as apologies. This went on for almost two hours. Then he finally went to sleep.

I was leaving at 8.30am. Even in London, then, Sunday morning travel took far longer than at any other time of the week, and I wanted to arrive at my interview in plenty of time.

I've said before that Tom's modus operandi was to prevent me from sleeping for hours and then he would sleep most of the following day. So I was very surprised when he was in the hallway ready to say goodbye to me as I left. He put his arms around me; I did not reciprocate. He apologised. He pleaded his case for how good we were together again. I said I had to go but we could talk later. And I left.

It was the last time I saw him.

It wasn't the last contact, though.

I was told by mutual friends that he had started seeing Nicky. She had demonstrated where her loyalties lie, so I was not too bothered about not hearing it from her. I heard she had moved in quite quickly. He was obviously a very persuasive man, as he had persuaded me quickly, too.

A few months later I had to go for a smear. I'm at high risk for cervical cancer; I've had pre-cancerous cells more times than I remember now. While I was in the surgery, the doctor asked if I wanted to be tested for STDs too. Being the responsible sort of person I am, I thought, well, I might be seeing a new man soon, and I would like to be able to say I've been tested and I'm all clear, so I agreed.

I hadn't had sex with anyone but Tom our whole relationship, and I hadn't had sex since it ended, so it was a surprise when I got a call to say that I had HPV.

I wrote to him to tell him. I didn't angrily confront him, saying he had obviously cheated on me; I didn't speculate in the letter whether it was his ex before me, who frequently made it clear she wanted him back, or if it was the woman he was flirting with at the nightclub, the night I decided I had had enough, or whether it was someone else. I just wanted to tell him so that he was aware, so he could get treatment, so he didn't infect anyone else. I did hope for an explanation though.

I didn't get one. I got a brief note written back:

Nicky's already got it so we're okay.

And that was that. My last contact with him.

What did I learn? Not much immediately, but over time, things started to become more apparent.

When I made the decision that I was leaving Tom, I told myself that I would rather be single for the rest of my life than spend another moment with him, but I really didn't think I would be single for that long.

I was very wrong about that!

I had a couple of dates with a couple of men, but nothing got further than a few fumbled kisses. I wasn't ready. I was too scared to get close to a man; I didn't know who I could trust, including myself, as my judgement had felt so poor.

I didn't realise at the time that I needed to work on myself. I needed to talk about all the things that had happened to me. I couldn't form a loving, trusting, relationship with someone else if I couldn't trust myself, if I didn't even like myself.

Oh! I got the job, though! Even with only two-and-a-bit hours of sleep, I was still a bloody good nanny.

End of chapter note: How are you feeling? Perhaps it's time for another do something lovely for yourself break?

Chapter Fourteen

A fool's kiss

"Never let a fool kiss you or a kiss fool you." — *Mardy Grothe*

When I said to myself that I was going to leave Tom, I told myself that I would rather be single for the rest of my life than spend another minute in a relationship with him, but I really didn't believe I would be single for long, as I never had been before. I was feeling a bit of pressure to meet THE ONE and HAVE BABIES!!! But I had also barely learned how to be a single adult; I wasn't sure I knew how to do it. And being single felt like I was a failure; my worth was tied up in being in a relationship, even though, in reality, my worth had been shot further to pieces by a partner.

Becoming newly single had coincided with me starting the final year of my degree, as well as doing two part time jobs a week, and commuting over 200 miles to do them both, so finding someone to do the horizontal dance with was not a priority. On nights out with friends (I could have as many of those as I could fit in now! Doing things that were more me, and absolutely no heavy metal gigs or bars), I would occasionally meet men but, with my confidence being so low, I never believed they were interested in me.

I always volunteered to drive so that I wouldn't get pressured into drinking; I had stopped drinking again, having been reminded that I only wanted to drink when I was feeling sad, but, as a student, I didn't feel brave enough to say I was teetotal. I felt like

I would be judged as a weirdo, or someone with ISSUES, if I admitted I didn't drink. Obviously, I did have ISSUES, big ones, but I didn't want people to know about them!

Anyway, I would meet these men, and I would feel they had no interest in me; I was too fat, ugly, boring, worthless; what did I have to offer? But, when they got drunk, I would allow their advances; I know it sounds ridiculous, but in my head, if they made advances when they were sober, it was out of pity; if they made advances when they were drunk, it meant their standards had dropped considerably so I probably made the grade. There were kisses and fumbles but never anything more. The thought of being seen naked scared me, but the thought of being seen when they were sober scared me even more.

So, I was single for the whole of my final year, and I was okay with that because, once I stopped university, I would have more time. I knew I was lying to myself though; I knew I was getting increasingly scared to be intimate with anyone again.

Until James, that was.

I met James when we were both studying on an Access Course that was aimed at giving mature students a recent qualification to get into universities, so he was before Tom. I was in awe of him. He was not like the men I'd met before. He had long hair, piercings, and was obviously from a very posh family; oh! His voice! It was deep and rumbly, and I felt it everywhere! He was also a few years younger than me, which felt a little dangerous, exciting. I loved how ethical he was; a vegetarian who boycotted companies due to animal testing; he protested on environmental issues. He seemed brave and exciting!

A few of us would regularly go to the pub after our evening classes, and as he was sort of (not really) on my way home, he would ask for lifts. He would always invite me in for a cup of tea; he introduced me to Earl Grey! That felt very fancy!

One night, a couple of weeks after starting our twice a week ritual, he asked if he could kiss me. He asked!!! Well!! That was an incredibly enticing offer! We kissed for a long time, and it was wonderful! Then I went home. This continued: take him home, Earl Grey tea, kissing, me going home, for a couple of weeks; then he asked if I would lie with him on his bed. His single bed! He was barely 20 and living at home with his parents. I was only a size 12 then, and he was svelte, so we fitted comfortably.

He had been reassuring me for weeks that he found me attractive and that he had imagined me naked many times; I doubted that he found me attractive, but I didn't doubt that he had imagined me naked. I had been taught from a young age that all men did was imagine women naked. The cynicism.

The sex was good, and he was attentive. But we were never a couple. It never came up in conversation, but we both knew that this was a friendship with benefits.

I had assumed that none of his friends knew about me and that he would never introduce them to me. However, sometimes a friend would pop by once we were back at his (it was after 9pm! How liberal and exciting to have friends just pop by at all hours!), and we would all chat. I felt quite flattered. He wasn't ashamed of me and our dirty little secret! I hadn't told my friends at first, feeling they would judge me.

However, I learned very quickly that I wasn't part of the equation at all. James was a dealer of Class B drugs. A posh boy like him! His "friends" didn't care whether I was there or not; they just wanted what James was offering. I will admit it was all a bit exciting. I was always a "goody two shoes". My family had constantly criticised me for not drinking, my sisters were smokers; yet, here I was, in a den of iniquity! I was curious but never tempted. The thought of being entirely relaxed was tempting, but my fear of losing control completely outweighed any temptations.

Our series of one night stands continued for most of the academic year. I'd occasionally dream about it becoming more serious, but I knew we never would be.

Once we didn't have a reason to meet regularly, our contact dwindled. The occasional phone call (his voice! Oh my!), a rare meet in person, then he went off to university and I continued in the job I was in in London. Even though I had done very well on the Access Course, I didn't believe I was good enough to go to university; I thought my marks were pity marks. Our conversations got even more infrequent.

Then I met Tom, and you know that part.

After leaving university but still living with the family I was working for in Bristol, James called out of the blue. It was lovely to hear him again.

He asked if he could come and visit. As it happened, the family were going to be away for a night, so I suggested he came then.

I had put on so much weight with Tom that I felt embarrassed. I told James that I was bigger. I was apologetic about it. He responded that that just meant there was more of me to love. My heart swelled but I believed he was just laying on the charm. It did feel good, though.

The excitement! The day he was going to arrive, I spent hours making it look like I hadn't spent hours getting me and the house ready for him.

He arrived, we hugged, he told me I looked beautiful, I made us dinner, we chatted.

Then I showed him to his room. I had thought he might find me repulsive now so I didn't want to assume he would want to sleep with me. I told him where my room was.

Then I sat on my bed, hoping he would come knocking, in more ways than one, but he didn't. To me, this was confirmation of how repulsive I was. I was devastated and validated. What I believed was obviously true.

The next day, he returned back to whichever part of the country he was living in then, after a long hug goodbye.

Several months later, when I was back in London, living in a wonderful flat that was a perk of being tempted back to nannying by my favourite family, he got in touch again. Can he come visit?

He came, we hugged, we talked, I cooked dinner. Then he reached out to play with my hair. I felt like I was melting. In a feat of bravery, I said that I didn't think he was interested in me, after our night in Bristol. He would never not be interested in me, he said, always the charmer. But, he said, there's a few things that are a bit different about me now; I have more piercings.

I couldn't see said piercings.

GULP!

He's the only man I have slept with who had *that kind* of piercings; I certainly wouldn't rule it out in the future.

Later that night, he left to go and see his family. Again, I knew it was nothing more than another one night stand with the same person.

I didn't see him again for several years. Seven to be precise.

In those seven years, which you have read about in other chapters, I moved back to my birth city, had several jobs, got very ill, physically and mentally, and stopped working.

And I had remained single. I had met a few men, but I was too scared to pursue anything, not that any of them appealed overly much. I was too scared to be alone with a man, too scared to trust anyone, too scared to trust myself.

Then James called. He said he was going to be house sitting for his aunt and uncle not far from me, so could he visit? He came to my little flat, we chatted, and it felt like it hadn't been so long. He'd had some mental health issues, and I was still living with mine (so was he but he hid them well then).

We kissed; that felt very familiar!

He said he had to leave but invited me over to stay with him the next night. There was that fear again! But I said yes. I had to say yes. My very loud insecurities were yelling at me, "NOOOOOOOOOO!" but I really wanted to be with him again.

He collected me the next night and took me to his temporary house. Through my nanny work, I have lived and worked in some very fancy houses; this house made those look like they weren't quite grown up yet. It was stunning! (You know when you have those if I win the lottery daydreams? This would be the house I would buy!) And it felt really homely. There were magazines and books piled high; things just left where they were put down, rather than put away; it felt comfortable. And there was a hot tub in the garden!!

That hot tub was wonderful! And, after seven years of celibacy (yes, James was the last person I'd had sex with), I remembered that sex with some people can be fantastic! And uncomfortable! I gripped the side of the hot tub with my upper arms so much, I had bruises for days.

I stayed the night, and we had a lovely time. He dropped me home the next morning and arranged to visit the next night. He did, and he stayed.

We had wonderful conversations about all sorts of things, including our mental health. Although we had shared many enjoyable evenings over the 14 or so years we had known each other, this was the night I felt closest to him; this was the night I thought there could be more.

The next night I saw two friends. I told them all about him. Both were quite judgemental that I had been having sex with a man for years with no commitment. I told them I thought I had fallen in love with him.

I wrote him a letter. I waffled. I apologised. I told him I thought I might love him.

And I never heard from him again.

This was devastating for a short period of time. Then I realised that I was in love with the idea of him but not really him. In all the years I had known him, we never actually knew each other all that well; I had imagined him to be this ethical philanthropist. I had imagined him to be this wonderful, loving, human who accepted who I was, at my size. The key word being imagined. I had imagined what I thought was my ideal man. That wasn't James (was it anyone?). I wanted it to be him. I wanted to believe that the man I imagined existed, and it was easier to think it was him. Maybe I was protecting myself from meeting other men; maybe I thought I was safer with him, with the idea of him, than I was with other men. I don't know.

Once I got over my temporary heartbreak, though, I realised that I had really missed being in a relationship, and sex, and I was ready to find it again.

End of chapter note: We're coming to the end of the difficult stuff; it gets happier soon.

Chapter Fifteen

Choosing life

"Today I choose life. Every morning when I wake up I can choose joy, happiness, negativity, pain… To feel the freedom that comes from being able to continue to make mistakes and choices – today I choose to feel life, not to deny my humanity but embrace it." — Kevyn Aucoin

Having read this far, it probably won't surprise you when I say I have mental health conditions. I have learned to live with them, and I have learned how to deal with the difficulties they throw at me. It isn't always easy, but I know my life is now better because of the techniques I use. In Positive Psychology terms, it means I have had Post Traumatic Growth — doesn't it feel fancy when you find out something you have been doing has a proper science-y name?!

My main ones are: Emotionally Unstable Personality Disorder/Borderline Personality Disorder (EUPD/BPD) — a.k.a Difficult Life Syndrome; Hypervigilance; mild OCD; and C-PTSD. That's quite a collection, isn't it?

The NHS definition of EUPD/BPD is:

> Symptoms of borderline personality include being emotionally unstable, having upsetting thoughts and acting without thinking.

The main treatment for borderline personality disorder is a type of talking therapy called psychotherapy.

The cause of borderline personality disorder is unclear. It's been linked to traumatic events during childhood, such as neglect or abuse.
(https://www.nhs.uk/mental-health/conditions/borderline-personality-disorder/overview/)

C-PTSD (Complex Post Traumatic Stress Disorder) has many of the same symptoms. We're so rarely treated holistically that, sometimes, we end up with a collection of diagnoses, when, perhaps, we might not have them all, but, rather, one or two that will encompass everything.

Whether it's BPD or C-PTSD, or both, don't they sound jolly.

I have that.

It's a difficult diagnosis to talk about, partly because of the stigma attached to it (the murderers in so many crime dramas are committed by people with BPD; so far, I've not murdered anyone). And partly because BPD is one of the "catch-all" names given when medical professionals have given up trying to find a potentially more suitable one.

I was diagnosed with it around 2013/2014, though I've lived with it for far longer.

The answer to why I have it, you can probably glean from the previous parts of my story in this book. I would much prefer the condition to be more widely known as "Difficult Life Syndrome". It's semantics, but when words like "unstable", "borderline", and "disorder" are used, they feel more dangerous, more volatile, and scarier. Whereas, "Difficult Life Syndrome" does what it says on the tin. I have this condition because I've had a difficult life.

How does it affect me?

I have been told many times that I am "high functioning"; that I can't possibly have it that bad because people don't see the same in me as they do in other people.

The thing is, partly because of the stigma attached to the condition, but mostly because of the life I've lived, I have become an expert at masking it, because that was the safest thing for me to do. If ever they give out Oscars for long-term acting while living, one of them will have my name on it.

But it affects every day, every hour, of my life.

Part of the condition for me is hypervigilance.

This means that I do these things:

• Every time I walk past the front and back doors, I have to check to ensure they're locked so it's harder for an intruder to break in. That's the thought I have every single time I pass the doors.

• Every time there's a knock on the door, anxiety swells within me, wondering if this is the time the person knocking is here to break in, rape, or murder me. Or all three.

• Every time I walk past a plug socket, if it's not being used, I have to switch it off because I have a fear of there being a fire.

• Every time I get up at night for a wee, I have to turn on the light in each area I pass through, and check behind the shower curtain, to ensure no one has broken in. I hold my breath the whole time.

• Every time I see a notification on my social media, or my emails, I worry that I've done something wrong, or that someone is going to tell me how rubbish I am.

- Every time I post in a group and I don't get a notification of someone interacting with it, I have to fight the thoughts that it's because nobody likes me.

- Every time I am in a room with other people, I have to do regular surveys so that I know who is there, who is getting too close, who I don't feel I can trust.

- Every time I use public transport, I regularly scan my fellow passengers as a risk assessment.

- Every time I walk anywhere, I am constantly checking who is around me and monitoring how safe I feel.

And I do mean every single time.

I also have frequent bad dreams. When I say I'm not good in the mornings, people make jokes, implying I'm lazy. I make some excuse about my night-time medication not wearing off quickly. In truth, I don't get that hazy, slow wake up feeling. Once I'm awake, I'm AWAKE!!! I'm aware of everything around me, sounds, sights, smells. I'm aware of the pain there is in my body immediately. And then I have to begin the transition from a night of vivid dreams to a day where I am constantly alert. I need that quiet time; without it, I am exhausted, and I feel vulnerable because I don't feel as alert. On occasions, I will do something before 10am, but it takes me a couple of days before I feel like me again.

I know there will be people reading this who know me, and these things will come as a surprise to them because I am high functioning. They will be surprised that happy, confident Vie has moments of anxiety before every single interaction in every single day. It's why I get "peopled-out"; I love being around people (now), but it is so tiring, and I really need, and value, my days when I am alone.

Some of the list above will make sense to some of you reading this; for others of you it won't. I will explain how it feels, then I will explain how I deal with it.

- *Every time I walk past the front and back doors, I have to check to ensure they're locked so it's harder for an intruder to break in. That's the thought I have every single time I pass the doors.*

I had a robbery in one of the apartments I lived in, but I wasn't home when it happened; that could be part of it continuing, but the issues have been there since before that happened. Even though most of the danger I faced was in the homes I was inside, I, like many children of my generation and, possibly, those since, had been taught about "stranger danger".

I have known for quite some time that most of the dangers we were expecting to happen with strangers were more likely to happen with people we knew/loved but, as a child, I thought that the dangers inside some of the houses I was in were really scary, so it must be much worse if a stranger was doing it! By checking the doors regularly, it made me feel that home was safer. It still makes me feel that way.

- *Every time there's a knock on the door, anxiety swells within me, wondering if this is the time the person knocking is here to break in, rape, or murder me. Or all three.*

As I've just said, no one has ever broken in when I have been at home, gratefully! I don't know if it's a continuation of the "stranger danger" thought process, or that, now I feel safe in my home, there's something in the inner workings of my brain that tells me I can never feel fully safe. What I do know is that, in the 16 to 20 steps it takes to walk to our front door from the sofa, or to run down the stairs from the office (we live in a small, terraced house; there's not much room for running long distances!), I have envisioned how the person on the other side of the door might rush inside, push me against a wall, hold a knife to my throat, then rape and/or murder me, before stealing from us, and then I nearly always open the door with a bright and cheery "hello".

- *Every time I walk past a plug socket, if it's not being used, I have to switch it off because I have a fear of there being a fire.*

I have a false memory of being in a fire. Even though it's false, the memory feels incredibly real. In the memory, we are being herded out of a Woolworths (remember those? Which was your favourite bit? I loved buying my singles from there.) that was on fire. My youngest sister had not been born at that time, so it was me, my middle sister, and our parents; my sister was sat on my dad's shoulders, and I was holding on to my mum's hand. I can remember the heat and the smell. Bizarrely, Benny Hill, the comedian, is in the memory, but, to be fair, we frequently saw him walking around the area of the memory with his Woolworths carrier bag.

Although this didn't happen, I have been in a fire that I have no recollection of: when I was a toddler, I was sat in the back seat of my dad's car; this was before the days of car seats or seat belts, or even worrying about leaving a toddler alone in a car where they weren't supervised. My parents were up a garden path, talking to a relative at their front door, and the car "exploded" (obviously it didn't, as I wouldn't be here to tell the tale, but you have probably gathered by now, my family have a sense of the dramatic). My dad pulled me out of the burning car.

So, fire scares me. Many years ago, I saw a programme about how turning off all unnecessary plugs at night helped limit fires happening; my brain, though, always having to go that one step further, has to turn off every socket as soon as I am finished with it, and I check them all several times a day.

• *Every time I get up at night for a wee, I have to turn on the light in each area I pass through, and check behind the shower curtain, to ensure no one has broken in. I hold my breath the whole time.*

This is similar to the previous one where I have fears of someone breaking in. I've never seen the film *Psycho*, and I've never seen the infamous shower scene, but I still worry that someone is going to stab me through the shower curtain. And, to potentially sound slightly more normal, there might be a giant spider in the bath. I don't like spiders.

• *Every time I see a notification on my social media, or my emails, I worry that I've done something wrong, or that someone is going to tell me how rubbish I am.*

Part of having BPD is an intense fear of abandonment. Because of this fear, many of us with the condition try to be the BEST FRIEND EVER!!! We try to make ourselves invaluable; we will be there to listen, to support, whenever you need us. This enthusiasm to be the best friend may seem childish to others but, for many of us, we have been rejected and abandoned so many times in our lives that that fear is utterly ginormous. So we will do what we can to not be rejected; we will be who you need us to be.

And then life happens, and abandonment is sometimes part of that; friends move away or move on; jobs change; relationships change; and we see everything as our fault. We think, if I had done this, they wouldn't have done that, or, if I hadn't said that, perhaps they would still like me. We blame ourselves all too easily; there have been times in my life when I could justify why a child falling over in a country several continents away was entirely my fault; unfortunately, that is not an exaggeration.

If anything went wrong anywhere, I could convince myself I was to blame. Although I am far better at dealing with these things now, having come a long way in my healing process, these feelings still leave an imprint on every interaction I have.

When I see people in person, it's easier; I can sense mood, the general feeling, and, with being hypervigilant, I have a superpower of being able to see and hear things other people miss, so I can tell when things have gone well. In the realms of the internet, though, I can't use my superpower so much, and so much goes on that I can't see, which means those little goblins in my brain try to come out to party and to have a bitch-fest, where I am the one they're bitching about. They'll tell me things like, "You shouldn't have just liked that status because now they don't think you care"; "You shouldn't have responded with a heart on that status because now they think you are a suck up"; "You shouldn't have made that joke on their post because now everyone will know you're not funny"; "You shouldn't have…." And those thoughts can be so frequent that you're always waiting for someone to tell you how rubbish you are; expecting someone, everyone, to tell you that you are worthless.

When you have spent a large part of your life being told that you are worthless, it's not too hard to believe that everyone would agree. With social media being the land of trolls, it's not hard to believe that you are an easy target because you nearly always have been.

- *Every time I post in a group and I don't get a notification of someone interacting with it, I have to fight the thoughts that it's because nobody likes me.*

We can sometimes feel that we need high numbers of friends and followers across our social media platforms; this will prove how popular we are: Look! Look at all these people who want to know what I am doing!! I must be likeable! What really happens though, is that having more people there means there are more people who will ignore you. I don't mean they are doing it deliberately, but those little goblins in my brain are determined to make it seem personal. They'll be telling me that no one is responding because I am boring and that I have nothing interesting to say. They'll be telling me that I am worthless, so why would anyone bother with me. Those goblins are really irritating little buggers.

- *Every time I am in a room with other people, I have to do regular surveys so that I know who is there, who is getting too close, who I don't feel I can trust.*

This makes me really tense. I'm not someone who relaxes much anyway, but situations like this can make me feel like Ram-Man in the He-Man cartoons (you may need to Google him). He was short and square, always ready for a fight, and was often used to break down doors; he always looked really tense! Not surprising really. In a room of people, even if it's people I know well, I always feel tense, and I feel like I am all hunched up, ready to be carried away and launched into something using my head, my body, as a battering ram.

Like many women, even ignoring the abusive relationships I have had in my life, I have been sexually assaulted in public places; I have had men, including gay men and sometimes drunk women, grab me and grope me; I've had men position their swollen dicks against me and rub. Having lived in environments where my body was just considered to be there for someone else's enjoyment or to berate, I have gone into freeze mode, from fight, flight or freeze, every time such an assault has happened. So the hypervigilant part of me goes on to high alert, looking out for situations where that could happen; looking for ways to escape if I need to.

- *Every time I use public transport, I regularly scan my fellow passengers as a risk assessment.*

This is similar to the last point, in that there have been too many (one is too many!) incidents where men have taken what they have seen as opportunities. Because of my paternal grandfather, I had a fear of thin, older men for a long time; having one of them sit next to me on a bus terrified me. The same was true of men with bad teeth (the abusing uncle had horrible teeth). Smells are incredibly evocative; if I could smell anything that would remind me of them, it would send me into a panic.

I have been on public transport when acts of violence have happened, when assaults have happened, when weapons, such as large rocks, have been thrown through windows. Imagine a meerkat, high on a hill, being the lookout for their mob (I've just looked up what the collective term was; every day's a school day), looking left, right, eyes always darting around; that's me.

- *Every time I walk anywhere, I am constantly checking who is around me and monitoring how safe I feel.*

Again, much the same as the previous two points, but with the added danger of not knowing where potential attacks could come from as everyone is moving in different directions. We're all taught about stranger danger from a young age and, even though I know from lived experience that most assaults happen with someone we know, it doesn't stop the very real concern when out in public. An addition to this is if I am in, or near, my hometown, and there's the possibility that I could bump into my family. I really don't want to bump into them, but if it is going to happen, I would much rather see them first so that I can either go in a different direction, or at least prepare myself for the potential conversation.

Goodness! If all this sounds exhausting to you, let me tell you that it's so much more so living it.

But! Hooray! There are ways that I have learned to deal with these things.

• Most of the time now, when I check that the doors are locked, I can tell myself that I am just checking because that's the sensible thing to do; the troubling thoughts of worrying about someone breaking in can be calmed with logic. I can tell myself that it's unlikely that someone will break in, especially if we are being safety conscious and ensuring the doors are locked.

• Although the fear of danger when someone knocks on the door is still present, now I can use logic to tell myself that this has never happened to me before ('Yes', those of you who also have similar thoughts will possibly think, 'but what if the law of probability suggests that the more time you go without it happening, the closer you are to it happening for real?!'). And I can tell myself that I am strong enough to fight back now; I can tell myself that I know I am not worthless and that I am worth fighting for; and, as I usually have a pen and/or a phone in my hand, I can always prod them with that or hit them on the head with this. The thoughts are still there but, I feel more able to deal with them now.

• Although I still turn plug sockets off that I am not using, such as the one for the toaster, the kettle and the oven once I have finished with them in the morning, I am okay with them being on all day when my partner is home. I have reasoned with myself that, in the unlikely event of something happening, we will be home so we can deal with it rapidly.

- How do I now deal with getting up in the night? In the many years my partner and I have been living together, he has only stayed away from the house one night (it's more likely that I am away visiting friends or attending events); if I am out of bed for longer than a few minutes, he notices I am not there. Also, our house isn't huge so I know that, even if my brain goes into freeze and I can't scream, I can knock something off a shelf, and he will hear. I also have extraordinary confidence that our cats will alert him to any issues, while also knowing that they might just get annoyed their sleep is disturbed. I know that may not seem like I have dealt with it but, in comparison to what it was, it's much better! There have been so many nights where I have just waited in bed, desperate for a wee but too scared to leave the bed until there is light; now, I wake up, get up, go, and get back; it takes four minutes from waking up to being back in bed.

- Social media and email notifications still cause anxiety, and I'm not sure it will ever stop; however, now, rather than instantly assuming I have done or said something wrong, I now believe in myself and I like who I am. I am also willing to accept responsibility if I'm wrong; so, although I still get these anxious thoughts, I can now tell myself that if someone is being unnecessarily difficult, which is a rare event, I know it's their problem and I am not responsible for their feelings.

- How do I deal with lack of interaction with my social media posts? When I was performing burlesque, then because of other things I was involved in, my Facebook friends list became huge, with almost 4,000 people; I would post something and, sometimes, there would be hundreds of likes; other times, there would be only a few; and I would get really upset. That lack of interaction increased my sense of worthlessness. It exacerbated my belief that I had nothing of value to say.

Then, as my confidence grew, and as I became more aware of the site's algorithms, I realised that having that number of people on my friend's list didn't mean I was going to get more interactions; it meant there were just more people that my posts wouldn't be seen by. It had absolutely nothing to do with me. Yes, sometimes, when I am tired, when I am tearful, the sadness about feeling ignored lingers, but, nearly every time, I can remind myself that it's just the techy gremlins that are not putting my stuff out for people to see.

One thing that really helped, happened quite recently. I ran a Crowdfunder campaign to get my children's book, *Where Are We Going?* produced and printed; I posted several times a day on my profile, on my business page, across other groups, across all my social media. I felt I was being spammy; I thought everyone on my friends list and beyond were probably sick of me continually talking about it. The night before the campaign ended, I sent a message to friends I thought would have supported, to give them a gentle nudge that the campaign was ending; I apologised for spamming and said I hope they understood why I had been posting so much. Nobody complained and several of them said, "I didn't know you had written a book!" It was a good reminder that so much of our social media lives is missed by so many — because of the algorithm.

• Do I still survey the room when I'm around a lot of people? Over the years of teaching myself ways to feel good about myself, ways to feel more confident, I can now happily be in a room and not feel I have to disassociate from myself (for many, many years, I felt I watched myself and my surroundings from up in a corner of the room; that I was there in body but the part of me that kept me safe hovered above, waiting to shout at me to GET OUT NOW!). Now, I believe in myself and believe that, should I feel uncomfortable, I can leave; and should anyone be the cause of that discomfort, depending on the type of discomfort, I have perfected the "Nanny glare" for those men who mansplain, and know I can challenge someone, loudly, if they think it is okay to touch my arse. I am still very aware of everything going on, but I am far more confident in my abilities to deal with the situation.

• How do I cope with public transport and just generally being out and about? (I felt these two would be best combined.) I have realised that, sadly, many women have to be vigilant when out because that's how we have learned to be safe. Some of us, like me, will be reading a book, or playing on our phones, giving off the "I'm busy" vibe; some will be talking loudly on speaker phone to let everyone know that they have someone on the other end who will notice if they are late; others will hunker down, earphones in, music loud, with an attitude that says, "This is my own private world; you stay away." Having been sexually assaulted a lot, I am possibly slightly more hypervigilant; unfortunately, I know that the majority of women have been sexually assaulted in some way or another, so the fear is very real in all of us.

Now, I feel less scared than I used to because, as I have already said, I feel more able to be loud in response to anything that may happen. I am also more willing to hurt someone who hurts me. In the past, I wouldn't have wanted to hurt someone; I would have felt guilty for inflicting pain on someone, even though they were harming me; the risk to my life was less important than the risk of hurting someone else. Ridiculous, huh? But that's how I felt. Everyone else, EVERYONE ELSE, was more important than me. Now, I know my value so I believe (we never know until we are faced with these situations) I would now make it very difficult for someone who tried to hurt me in such a way.

It's interesting how some (many?) of us have thoughts about what we feel we would do if someone we didn't know tried to assault us; we make plans; we feel slightly more prepared for "stranger danger". Yet, we don't prepare for if it's our loved ones, those who are closest to us, who are causing us pain, emotional or physical, even though, statistically, assaults are more likely to be carried out by someone we know.

I wonder if the thought seems so preposterous that we can't fathom it. Or if the thought of it causes so much fear that our brains automatically go into freeze mode.

For me, I believe I have done so much work on myself that I have faith in who I am and that I would tell a partner where to go if ever they made me feel unsafe.

But.

Then.

I imagine most of us would feel that way until it happens.

End of chapter note: Mental health issues are incredibly hard; there are organisations listed in the back of the book that you can turn to for help, should you need to.

Chapter Sixteen

Courage and strength

"Hard things are put in our way, not to stop us, but to call out our courage and strength." — Unknown

I also have physical disabilities. I was born with one, and I've collected more along the way.

When I was born, apparently, I had very raw skin on my bottom. No one looked into why, as it healed quite quickly.

Throughout my childhood, there were many ordinary childhood injuries — scraped knees and hands — that didn't heal the same way as other people's. There were times when my feet would get badly blistered from shoes, and blister when I had no shoes on. The blisters wouldn't be like the blisters most people get, like the ones that get rubbed on to a heel by a new pair of shoes; these blisters would be huge! They would engulf my toes and cover my heels. People are told not to pop blisters, as that increases the risk of infection, so my blisters would get bigger and bigger until they popped, or my mum decided it was worth risking infection. The blisters were always worse in the warmer months, April through to October.

My parents, my family, were not sympathetic.

On the rare occasion I got taken to see a doctor about it, the professional was lacking in any knowledge. I got told it was two different types of eczema and was told to soak my feet in potassium permanganate, which did nothing but turn my feet and nails brown and made me even more of a target for bullying (as if walking like a constipated chicken because of heavily blistered feet wasn't enough!).

I was told my skin was too soft on my feet, so I had to harden them up by being barefoot as much as possible. I got told the skin was too hard, so I had to wipe my feet with Surgical Spirit every night. Oddly, I still really like the smell of Surgical Spirit; I wonder if it's because using it was a rare act of self-care?

I got told I was allergic to my own sweat, and that I had to either stop sweating (!!!) or learn to live with it; I have always sweated a lot! Being told this was part of this painful issue added to my embarrassment and how useless I felt.

My parents never followed any of these up; there were never any demands to see a dermatologist; there were never questions as to why it was happening; why nothing was working.

I was always made to feel that it, that I, was an inconvenience and I was making my feet blister.

As a teenager, I got the train track braces on my top teeth. The orthodontist, a nice lady, did this work as a hobby; she spent most of her year travelling, especially skiing, which meant appointments were few and far between. The braces really hurt! Not only did they feel too tight on my teeth, but they made my mouth very sore too. The orthodontist said I was getting more ulcer type things than other patients, but that they would all be worth it once my teeth were fixed! (My teeth were only ever so slightly not straight.) My mum just told me it was something I had to put up with. I got through a lot of Bonjela Mouth Gel!

Once I left home, I could take myself to the doctor. Most of them had no clue either, but they would refer me to dermatologists. Eventually, I saw a dermatologist who took one look at my feet and said: "That's a prime example of Epidermolysis Bullosa Simplex Weber Cockayne!"

In a truly eloquent way, I went, Huh?"

There then followed a lot of words, many of which, as it was highly medicalised language, I had never heard before: genetic blah blah skin blistering blah blah no cure learn to live with it blah blah charity Debra.

I was none the wiser.

But it did feel good to have a name for it!

He then sent me off to the hospital's photography lab because he wanted photos of my feet for a dermatology medical journal. This was late 1998; if anyone happens to have a dermatology magazine with feet in from that era, I would love to see!

I went home and started to research. I couldn't find much, but I did find the charity.

All my life I had felt, had been told, that I was a freak. I had never met anyone with the condition, and the doctors I saw had no clue what the issue was. On top of an already lonely childhood, this had all added to it. Once I started having boyfriends, I would try to hide my feet as frequently as I could, embarrassed for them to be seen. The only time I was happy to have my feet seen was when I was with the children I looked after; they would look, ask questions, I would answer as best I could, which at the time was with very little, and then they would carry on with what they were doing. No judgement.

But, once I started learning more about the charity, I learned that I was not alone in all of this. I was part of a community I hadn't known existed! I belonged somewhere!

When I was a child, an uncle gave me an old briefcase record player and I would play my parents' singles from their teenage years and dance around my shared bedroom. One of my favourite songs, then and now, was "Downtown" by Petula Clark. I loved the whole song but the lyrics that lodged in my heart were these:

And you may find somebody kind to help and
understand you

Someone who is just like you and needs a gentle
hand to

Guide them along.

So maybe I'll see you there

We can forget all our troubles, forget all our cares

So go downtown

Things will be great when you're downtown

Don't wait a minute more downtown

Everything is waiting for you

Downtown. (Downtown. Petula Clark. Writer: Hatch
Anthony Peter)

Through finding the charity, Debra, I felt like I had found others
like me who would help and understand.

I started to meet others with EB (much easier to say than
Epidermolysis Bullosa!). I made friends and learned so much
about my condition. It was incredible! A condition that people
had dismissed, that had made me feel isolated, was now bringing
me knowledge and friendships I had never expected to find.

I began to learn more about the condition. The NHS explanation
of EB, and the symptoms they state, are:

> Epidermolysis bullosa (EB) is the name for a group
> of rare inherited skin disorders that cause the skin to
> become very fragile. Any trauma or friction to the
> skin can cause painful blisters.

The main symptoms of all types of EB include:

- skin that blisters easily
- blisters inside the mouth
- blisters on the hands and soles of the feet
- scarred skin, sometimes with small white spots called milia
- thickened skin and nails.

(https://www.nhs.uk/conditions/epidermolysis-bullosa/)

Even though it is a genetic condition, I am the only one in my family with it. I have been told I am a mutant — I am still waiting for Wolverine (well, Hugh Jackman; can you imagine the damage those claws could do to my fragile skin?! ;-)) to come calling.

I have learned that there are several varieties of EB; mine is one of the "lesser" ones. I say lesser, but even in its lesser forms, it still affects every level of our lives. Here are some of the ways it affects me:

- I have to be very careful about what I eat. I can't eat anything spicy, peppery, acidic, hard, or sharp. That means I can't eat most salad leaves (too peppery); I can't eat most fruit (too acidic); I shouldn't eat crisps or hard sweets. The spicy, peppery, and acidic foods cause my mouth to blister; the hard and sharp foods tear my mouth. Sometimes, my throat can blister too. Any blistering or tears makes any eating difficult and painful.

- My hands. If I hold a pen or pencil for too long, my skin shears. Opening up bottle tops causes my hands to shear. Wearing rings can create raw patches. If I iron, my hands shear and blister (obviously, a great reason to not bother ;-)). Holding anything for any period of time, such as knives, potato peelers, most kitchen implements, causes the skin on my palms to become raw.

- Shoes. I have to think carefully about the shoes I wear; heat and friction are causes of my blisters, so I can't wear shoes that will make my feet too hot; I can't wear shoes that have too many straps or edges (it's so painful taking shoes off when blisters have formed around straps). I can't wear shoes that put pressure on a particular point of my foot. Well, that should be "I shouldn't wear"; I do love a good pair of high heels every now and then, but I suffer for it.

- My feet. You know how uncomfortable it is to get a stone in your shoe. My feet feel like that most of the time. Generally, my feet feel like I have stones under the skin; on bad days, it feels like my skin has been torn open with a rusty razor blade, had lava shoved in, then sewn back up with a blunt needle. This makes walking on any ground hard, but it's especially hard on uneven ground, shingle, pebbles and other rough ground.

- Itching. My skin itches All. Of. The. Time. Sometimes, I can ignore it, maybe just having a good scratch now and then. When it's bad, I would happily tear my skin off and rub it vigorously on a cheese grater. Maybe I do need Wolverine.

- My body. Although it's mostly my mouth, hands and feet that are affected by my EB, I can blister anywhere, anywhere where there is any heat and/or friction. You know how, sometimes, when we sit down, our clothes can get a little twisted around us? I did that wearing trousers once and, because the seams ended up being tight against my legs, as most of the fabric got caught under me, my thighs blistered. I, thankfully, don't blister too often on my thighs, but it has happened when holes have appeared in tights, too. Thankfully, when I self–harmed, I rarely caused blisters.

People with EB Simplex make up around 70% of the EB community across the world, but very few of us have exactly the same symptoms. This condition really does have an impact on how we live every day.

Many of my friends with EB have the more severe forms: Dystrophic and Junctional. The condition is far more impactful on their lives.

A lot of the marketing around fundraising for EB charities is about our skin being as fragile as a butterfly's wing; for many parents, this means they cannot pick up their children with EB with their hands, or play rough and tumble games, because this would cause huge damage to their skin.

For many people with dystrophic or junctional EB, their fingers and toes can become webbed because of the high levels of scarring.

Lots of them have to have frequent oesophageal dilations because their throats are so scarred that the windpipe becomes smaller; as my throat is blistering more and frequently, I worry that this may be in my future, too; gratefully, I have people who can guide me through it.

Some of the forms of EB are life threatening. People I have loved, from the age of two up to a friend in her 60s, have died due to complications of the condition: an infection, a skin cancer, something else. I won't work out how many people I have lost due to the condition because I fear the number will be too high to fully comprehend.

I have been asked by non-EB people why I stay so involved with the community when there is so much loss; I always answer, because there is far more joy. The EB community was the first family I felt part of; I love them.

End of chapter note: If you have an undiagnosed condition, please do push to get tests done. And please reach out to communities that will understand; there are some on social media platforms that are great for offering support.

Chapter Seventeen

Accomplishments

"The measure of a man, or woman, is not so much what they have accomplished, though that has weight. It often is much more though what that man or woman has overcome to accomplish what they have." — *Leif Gregersen*

I have other chronic conditions, too. I believe that some of them are a result of lack of treatment in my childhood.

I've had pain in my hips for around 20 years.

It took several years to I be diagnosed with bursitis.

The NHS definition of bursitis is:

> Bursitis is when your joints become painful, tender and swollen. It can usually be treated at home and should go away in a few weeks.

> Bursitis happens when the fluid-filled sacs (bursa) that cushion your joints become inflamed.

> You might have bursitis if 1 of your joints is:

- painful – usually a dull, achy pain
- tender or warm
- swollen or red
- more painful when you move it or press on it

It can affect any joint, but is most common in the shoulders, hips, elbows or knees.

(https://www.nhs.uk/conditions/bursitis/)

Yeah. It "should" go away in a few weeks. As I said, I've had pain in my hips for around 20 years. According to the CDC: "Chronic diseases are defined broadly as conditions that last 1 year or more and require ongoing medical attention or limit activities of daily living or both"
(https://www.cdc.gov/chronicdisease/about/index.htm).

I'm also one of the "lucky" ones, in that I have it in more than just one joint; I have inflamed bursa in both my hips, groin, and buttocks.

For me, most days, the pain feels like I have an angry, demanding toddler, continually thumping me, wanting my attention. On bad days, it feels like someone is shoving some kind of trident fireside poker, scalding hot, into each inflamed bursa. Sometimes, because my body loves a jolly jape, it will be the manageable angry toddler, then, angry toddler suddenly turns demonic, thumping with fists of flames and spikes that unbalance me, then they'll smile sweetly and go back to the persistent, non-flamey, thumping.

This all adds to my difficulties with walking, standing, and, sometimes, even sitting. It's hard to get comfy when it feels like you have giant marbles in your posterior.

Over the years I have been given medication that, unfortunately, didn't work; to add to my curious cases of conditions, I am "delightfully" drug resistant. Most of the time, the drugs don't work (wasn't that a song?) or I become that one in a million on the prescription information leaflet. Previous incidents include me going from completely fine to acting as if I had been drinking gin for 12 hours straight, slurring my words and unable to stand straight, in the space of ten minutes, and being able to give a drunken lecture to my partner on fascinating facts about spiders because there was a spider on the wall. This is extra odd as, usually, I am arachnophobic. I've also blacked out and, at other times, had weeks where I was unable to sleep for more than 40 minutes at a time; thankfully, I did usually get back to sleep after a while, but the disturbed sleep was exhausting.

I have also had steroid injections in my hips. Again, no joy. And physio. And acupuncture. And massage...

I have been told my only option now is surgery, but the specialist I see has told me that the success rate is low and, right now, I don't want to put myself through that. There may come a time when I'll feel that's the best option, though. Just not now.

I also have endometriosis.

It wasn't diagnosed until around nine years ago, but I believe I have had it since puberty; that was over 20 years before I got diagnosed. That's actually not that uncommon.

This is what the NHS website says about endometriosis:

> Endometriosis is a condition where tissue similar to the lining of the womb starts to grow in other places, such as the ovaries and fallopian tubes.

> Endometriosis can affect women of any age.

It's a long-term condition that can have a significant impact on your life, but there are treatments that can help.

Symptoms of endometriosis

The symptoms of endometriosis can vary.

The main symptoms of endometriosis are:

• pain in your lower tummy or back (pelvic pain) – usually worse during your period
• period pain that stops you doing your normal activities […]
• difficulty getting pregnant

You may also have heavy periods. You might use lots of pads or tampons, or you may bleed through your clothes.

For some women, endometriosis can have a big impact on their life and may sometimes lead to feelings of depression.
(https://www.nhs.uk/conditions/endometriosis/)

And periods are usually so much fun, otherwise!

For me, thankfully, as with my EB, I have a "mild" form. This means that I am usually not affected most days, "just" for around ten days a month, with two to three hideous days.

On my bad days, I am exhausted. I don't mean I'm tired and could do with a nap; I mean EXHAUSTED. I mean that it feels like I am wading through setting concrete. I mean that a fork feels too heavy to lift to my mouth. I mean that the thought of standing and making lunch feels like climbing Kilimanjaro. I mean that having to concentrate so hard to be able to have a conversation with someone that, after, no matter how happy the conversation is, I just want to cry.

So, on saying all this, you would think sleeping would be easy, eh? I wish!! I'm in so much pain that it's difficult to settle. Then, because I am bleeding so heavily, I have to get up three or four times a night. Which adds to the exhaustion.

And the pain!!! I am in pain every single minute of every single day. But, when it's "that time", every single bit of pain intensifies and there's new pain on top!!

The bursitis pain I talked about, with the thumping and stabbing sensation, now also has a tearing sensation; it feels like every piece of muscle and tendon in my hips is tearing, desperate to get away from whatever it is attached to.

Other conditions that I haven't talked about yet are also exacerbated; my degenerative spinal disease, which normally means fairly constant backache, feels like I am being kicked continuously.

My thoracic outlet syndrome, which makes my hands and arms painful to use, is even more painful because of the aforementioned wading through concrete feeling.

And then, we have the "usual" period pains; for me, it feels like I have a lead rugby ball in my lower abdomen that some burly rugby player kicks every now and then for fun.

I try so hard to get comfortable, but each position only remains comfortable for a matter of minutes. Sometimes, you'll find me balanced precariously on the edge of the sofa, bent double; other times, I will be hanging over the edge of the arm of the sofa; occasionally, it feels better to have my knees tucked up close to my chest; or I might need to stretch and take up as much space as possible.

And I am one of the women where it has affected my fertility. Or lack thereof. As I mentioned in a previous chapter, I got pregnant once, when I was 22; I miscarried at 13 weeks, and I haven't been able to get pregnant since.

So, even for me, a "mild" case, endometriosis is not "just" a bad period. It's painful, emotional, and exhausting.

Another of my conditions is called thoracic outlet syndrome. It was diagnosed following an MRI, along with my degenerative spinal disease diagnosis. I'm going to go on record and say I HATE MRIs!!! It's like being squished in an aggressively squeaky toothpaste tube.

Anyway.

The NHS list of thoracic outlet syndrome symptoms is:

> • pain in your neck and shoulder, which spreads into your arm – this may be constant or come and go
> • temporary loss of feeling, weakness or tingling in the affected arm and fingers
> • temporary inability to carry out fine hand movements – such as doing up buttons [...]
> (https://www.nhs.uk/conditions/cervical-rib/)

For me, it's mostly in my left arm, with the rare bad day in my right arm.

Usually, it feels like I have a sharp pencil stabbing my elbows; my forearms feel as if a heavy weight has been dropped on them; the two outer fingers on each hand, and up to the knuckle on my middle finger, feel like they have cramp; there's also a constant stiffness in my left shoulder. I've gotten used to my hands and arms feeling like this, though it's not comfortable.

Then there's the days where I long for the stabbing and heavy feelings.

On those days, my elbows feel like they are being smashed; my forearms and wrists feel like they are being crushed in a vice; nearly the whole of my hands feel cramped and pained. It feels like I am being hit across my neck and shoulders with a cricket bat.

When it's bad like this, doing anything feels like I am fighting against treacle. As I said in chapter 13, 'It doesn't define me', with Tom, I did some bodybuilding, and, at my peak, I could deadlift more than my body weight; on the days when my thoracic outlet syndrome is bad, it feels like my arms are the heaviest weight I have ever lifted. This means that even using the body puff in the shower seems heavy; lifting a kettle is agony.

One of the most embarrassing things, though, is, if I am out for a meal and the cutlery is too heavy, or if it has any bumpy edges, my EB is exacerbated too, and I have to ask whoever is with me to cut my food. It's things like that that make me feel my independence is threatened.

As they were diagnosed at the same time, I shall talk about my degenerative spinal disease, too, although, really, medically, there's not too much to tell: my spine is slowly crumbling.

Whether it's because of the spinal disease, or a result of holding myself awkwardly due to all the other conditions, I always have a backache. It's mostly tolerable, thankfully. Then there's days where moving is excruciating. If my back is rested against something, like the back of the sofa, moving my limbs doesn't cause my back extra pain, but, as soon as I move away from that support, it's a searing pain that makes me feel nauseous. By the way, I have a phobia of vomit; apart from hating not feeling in control, if I vomit, because of my EB, the acid in it tears my mouth and throat apart. Feeling nauseous makes me anxious.

Another physical issue I have is peripheral neuropathy.

Peripheral Neuropathy is actually quite common; around one in ten people, over the age of 55 have it; having had it for several years, I had it a long time before that age, but it's nice to know that, eventually, I will have something that's quite common in my age group.

The NHS says this about it:

> The main symptoms of peripheral neuropathy can include:
>
> • numbness and tingling in the feet or hands
> • burning, stabbing or shooting pain in affected areas
> • loss of balance and co-ordination
> • muscle weakness, especially in the feet
>
> These symptoms are usually constant, but may come and go.
> (https://www.nhs.uk/conditions/peripheral-neuropathy/)

In all honesty, I sometimes can't tell if the symptoms I'm having are caused by peripheral neuropathy or thoracic outlet syndrome, or something else entirely. And, although I am incredibly grateful that I live in a country that has the NHS, I have found that the treatment I've received is compartmentalised. I am fairly sure that my bursitis, thoracic outlet syndrome, peripheral neuropathy, and degenerative spinal disease, are linked to walking wonkily for decades on blistered feet, but, because each condition affects a different body part, they get treated individually, rather than collectively.

It's always quite demoralising writing down your conditions. It's especially so when I have to complete the forms to continue receiving my disability benefit. I am sure those forms are designed to make people go into hibernation, too scared to breathe or move for fear of recrimination from the DWP. It seems they, the Department of Work and Pensions, have quite a Dickensian view of disability; it feels like they think we should be living in cesspits of our own fluids, barely able to talk or move, and, anything beyond that, YOU ARE FIT TO WORK! You fill in the form that gets judged by someone who has never met you; then you have an appointment with someone else who has never met you, and they ask you degrading questions, and then they make a judgement on how "fit" you are.

When I am completing the form, and around the assessment time, I have, well, I would say daydreams, but they're not particularly fluffy enough to be daydreams, so let's say imaginings. I think about getting all the DWP people that will be making decisions about me to have representations of my body: I would tape their feet up with varying size pebbles, to represent my EB, get an angry toddler to continually thump them in their hips, groin and buttocks to represent my bursitis, ask a huge rugby player to kick them sporadically in the stomach to represent my endometriosis, and have someone stabbing them in the elbows with a sharpened pencil all day, then occasionally trapping their arms in vices to feel the cramp, for my thoracic outlet syndrome. They would also have someone intermittently pour hot water from the kettle over their hands and feet to represent the peripheral neuropathy, have someone give them electric shocks with a cattle prod, to represent the spasms that I have in my back and hips (the reason, apparently, is that my brain has maladapted to the amount of pain I have, doesn't know what to do with it, so sends me spasms to make everything more painful. Thanks Brain). And that's just the physical conditions! To then add in the mental health conditions, well, I wonder how "fit for work" they would feel after a day living in my shoes.

Can you tell that I find these assessments incredibly stressful?

I've been referred to a pain clinic. The psychologist I saw there told me that they could do nothing for me because I already do everything they recommend; I make the best of my time when I am able; I try to find the joy in life; and I do what I can for my community. These are all great things, and, without doubt, they certainly make my life a far happier one, but it's not helpful when you would still like to receive help and support for the conditions you live with. And it's not helpful when being assessed by the DWP because finding joy in life allegedly means you are not disabled "enough".

And, though I am virtually unemployable, I do work. I wanted to make a contribution to society, so I set up my own business. And, because it's my own business, my boss is usually, though not always, quite good at giving me the time off I need to rest. It means that I can work the hours that suit me. It means I can do an hour here, 30 minutes there, whatever I feel up to at whatever time.

As I said, it's quite demoralising writing everything down. Although I don't forget I have all of these conditions (how could I?!), I do frequently ignore them, especially when I am involved in something. Have you ever done one of those guided mindfulness visualisations, where they ask you to think about every part of your body, bit by bit, so that you can see how it all feels? I know how it all feels, and my brain works really hard to try to not focus on them so I can continue to move.

I am also very grateful that I have a partner who has adapted to these changes in my body, and now does most of the housework.

End of chapter note: Take a deep breath. That's the hard stuff done! Now, we're moving into happier territory.

Chapter Eighteen

Love

"Hope for love, pray for love, wish for love, dream for love...but don't put your life on hold waiting for love." — Mandy Hale

I have been with my partner for over a decade. We don't have a perfect relationship, but we have a good one, and, for the first time in any relationship, I feel safe. And, importantly, he feels safe with me.

Feeling safe doesn't sound romantic or sexy but, my goodness! When you have lived a life in fear, it's the best thing!

I'll tell you a little about him; well, a little bit about our relationship, rather than him, as he is very private.

We actually met online, on the website Plenty of Fish (does that still exist?). We talked for several weeks before we even started planning to meet up. I had had several dates with different men, so I was almost blasé about it; I was close to giving up on finding "THE ONE" and was happy to have dalliances.

I arranged all of my first dates to be in the local art gallery. It's easy to get to, not too busy but not solitary. There's always the art to talk about if you run out of other things to say, and how someone views a piece is a good way of getting to know them a little better.

In our local gallery, there is the Perseus Series. When I was a child, despite coming from a family where many of them were creative, there was never really an appreciation of art. So, although the art in the Perseus Series is not a style I would choose to hang on my wall now, when I went there on a school trip as a child, it had a huge impact! It opened my eyes to the possibilities of what could be created.

Another important part of this particular gallery, for the purpose of my dates, was the painting "Atlas Turned to Stone" (all of the paintings in the series were painted by Sir Edward Coley Burne-Jones in the 1800s). In the painting, Atlas, in all his glory, is standing with the world on his shoulders. Because of his nudity, you can see the size of his penis. His penis is considered small by some. At the time of the painting being created, it was customary for warriors to be painted with large penises and academics to be painted with smaller ones.

On every date I went on, when we got to that painting, every man made a comment on the size of Atlas's penis; when I explained why, all of them would put their hands on their hips, slightly thrust them forwards, and say, "Well, I know which one I am!" I felt sure that deep inside their brains there was a little cave man shouting aggressively, "I am man! I am strong! I am warrior! I have big penis!"

Well, all of them but one said it.

This new man just went, "That's interesting!" He felt no need to thrust. He felt no need to imply his penis would make a horse jealous.

Then we carried on, talking more. And I thought, this man could be worth a second date. To be fair, I did frequently go on second dates, as I feel we all get nervous on a first date and possibly don't show our best sides; but, for this man, I felt he started well.

After several more emails back and forth, we arranged a second date. We had a lovely time, with some great conversations. I liked him but I didn't feel a spark. So, when he sent me an email saying that though he really liked me, he wasn't as ready for a new relationship as he had thought and would like to be friends, I was okay with that and thought it very unlikely that we would ever see each other again.

But we did. We actually started chatting more frequently, and he regularly came to visit; we would go out for dinner, to the cinema, to shows. He even came to my debut burlesque performance. He became a really good friend. So much so, that I would tell him about the dalliances I was having. I had decided that I was bored with dating and trying to find that special someone, so I actively sought out casual relationships where dinner and sex was all we were going to expect; I really enjoyed it! And I told my new good friend all about it because I didn't even think our relationship was going to be any more than a friendship.

Then, something changed.

Ten months after our first real life meeting, I was performing in his home city. We had arranged for him to meet me at the train station and that I was going to stay at his for the night. We had frequently shared my bed, platonically, when we had been out late somewhere, so this was nothing new.

But, the feelings I had when I saw him as I got off the train did feel new. As he walked towards me, I felt I should be running towards him, just like a 1940s film noir, throwing myself into his arms.

"Well, that's new", I thought.

When I get anxious, I chew on spearmint Soft Mints (other brands are available but they're my favourite), so I always had them with me when I performed (useless fact: when I was performing, if you Googled burlesque spinster Soft Mints, I will be top of the search!), but I had run out, so I was expecting to be able to get some before I got to the venue. We went to several shops but couldn't find any. This did not help my anxiety! I had to get to the venue, so I bought some not so good mints and he dropped me off.

He came back to the venue before it was officially opened. He had gone to several more shops until he had found my favoured mints, and he had bought lots!

"He is so lovely!", I thought.

He had come to the show alone and sat with a table of strangers, which I found impressive. During the interval, I left the dressing area and went to see him. I crouched by his side, and we were chatting away, and I thought,

"I want to kiss him." Then I thought, "That's a new thought!"

After the show, we went back to his. His housemate was away so he had arranged to sleep in their room, and I was going to have his room.

"Oh. I thought we would be sharing a bed," I thought.

The next day, although I had my train booked to return home, he suggested we spend the day together and that he would drive me home later. It was an unexpectedly beautiful spring day, we were by the sea, so it seemed like a great idea.

First of all, we walked up to the top of a cliff that had stunning views. As we got to the top, he looked over the edge and said,

"I don't want to, but I can see why people get the urge to jump."

"Nah, I don't," I said. "I get the urge to push."

Thankfully, he laughed.

We then began a walk along the seafront. I had brought clothes and a pair of boots that were perfect for the day before but far too warm for that day. My EB is exacerbated by heat and friction, so, as we walked, my feet grew increasingly blistered. I was getting very wobbly, so he took my handbag, put it over his shoulder, then gave me an arm to hold onto.

And we giggled a lot.

There was a film that we both wanted to see, so he suggested we watch it at his, as he had a far bigger TV than me, and then he would drive me home after. I don't do scary, for fairly obvious reasons shown throughout this book, but I had a curious fascination with this particular film (it's called *Antichrist*, if you're interested), so I said to him that I was happy to watch it but that he was not leaving me alone in my flat after watching it! He agreed. We watched the film. It was horrible. We drove back to mine, and we went to bed. Platonically.

He went home the next day.

I was due to have day surgery the following week, and I had my pre-op assessment that day. They asked me who my next of kin was; I had stopped seeing my family by this point, so I put down the name of the person I trusted most: him. I phoned him after to ask if that was okay, and I could hear the emotion in his voice. It was definitely okay.

Later that week, I met up with a friend who had spent time with us both. I told her about these new weird, slightly sparkly, feelings I was having about him. I bemoaned that the emotions were pointless because he only wanted to be friends.

She looked at me, with a look that told me how ridiculous she thought I was.

She said,

"He has been in love with you for months; everyone else has known for ages; it's just you that couldn't see it."

Being the intelligent, eloquent woman I am, I went,

"Oh."

He was due to visit the following weekend, as he was taking me to the hospital for my surgery and looking after me afterwards. I pondered over what I was going to say, if I was going to say anything at all.

The day before he was due to visit, we were chatting on the phone. I had decided I was going to say something, but I had no idea how or what. I had realised that I would rather know for sure if there was hope of a different kind of relationship, and I was prepared to lick my wounds if he said no.

I was attending writing classes at the time; my first short story had been published. I told myself I was good with words! I could do this! I could make it casual. I could make it seem relaxed, no big deal.

A natural break in the conversation. This was it! This was the chance I had to take!

"Hypothetically," I said, "if two friends had a great relationship, but one of them felt things had changed, how would you deal with that?"

Cool, casual, I thought; he won't suspect I'm talking about us!

"You're talking about us," he said.

So much for cool and casual!

I spluttered, "Yeah. I am."

He said,

"I've thought about this. It's like someone is offering you the juiciest, ripest, most delicious strawberry ever; do you take the strawberry, knowing that no other strawberry will ever live up to it? Or do you leave the strawberry and just be satisfied with not so good strawberries for the rest of your life?"

My eloquent response?

"You eat the fucking strawberry!"

"We'll talk about it tomorrow," he said, "and we'll take it slow."

The next day I made a veggie Bolognese in preparation. I'm a good cook, usually; that was the worst meal I ever made! And he was late (he got caught up in a family thing and didn't want to tell them why he wanted to rush away), which, rather than adding to flavour by allowing it to simmer, it added to the flavour by highlighting how awful it was.

We didn't take it slow.

And we've been together since.

It's not always easy, because most relationships aren't. But it's the best one I've had.

He has watched me continue to blossom; he has supported me in my adventures. He has talked period poverty to strangers when I was running a branch of a project that dealt with that issue. He has stood and person-ed a vegan hot dog stand for 10 hours when I was co-organiser of a large event in the city, as well as helping set up and close down. He has watched me give many public talks, been to shows and events that were not his thing, driven me to places and collected me from more, joined in at vintage events and the events I put on, embraced my love of Strongman competitions, and stood by me as my tiny business grows.

Yeah, it's not perfect, it may not last forever, like every couple, we argue and disagree sometimes, but most of the time, it's bloody good.

And I know I deserve that.

I feel safe enough to challenge him when we disagree, as he does me; I feel safe enough to tell him he has annoyed me. I feel safe.

As I said, safe doesn't sound sexy or romantic, but it really is.

And, after decades of abuse, trauma, and self-hatred, I know I am worthy of feeling loved, safe, cherished and adored.

We all are.

End of chapter note: I know there's been some hard stuff to get through; I hope you are okay. Remember there are organisations listed at the back of the book if you feel you need them. Now, on to living much more happily!

Part Two

*"What you do makes a difference, and you have to decide what
kind of difference you want to make." — Jane Goodall*

Chapter Nineteen

Beginnings

"And suddenly you know: It's time to start something new and trust the magic of beginnings." — **Meister Eckhart**

It was in 2010 that I decided I was ready to change my name.

At the time, I belonged to a writing group, and I wrote a piece to help explain why it was so important to me, hoping they would accept it and understand.

I thought I would share some of it with you here.

Lotus

I was born in the year that my birth name was the most popular; in every classroom there was always at least one other. I never felt like an individual; I was one of many.

The name never suited me; I never felt we belonged together. I hated it.

My mum gave me her name, a name she doesn't even like, as my middle name, because it was the "done thing". I have rarely used it as, with it, my initials would spell sag: a possible portent of my life. To sag is to droop, to curve under pressure. My name did not cause me to wilt, to never fully bloom, life did that, but it was certainly indicative of it.

My surname was the worst of all. It is astounding how many variations there could be when pronouncing so few letters. Most people would insist on saying the name, aggressively, like a violent furball in their mouths that they were desperate to be rid of.

The worst part of this name, though, is not how it sounds but what it means to me. It's my father's name, and his father's name. My father, who has been a continual emotional absence in my life; a man who runs and hides from issues, losing so much in the process, rather than feel what he needs to grow.

And his father. The man who has been the recurring nightmare in my life. The man who took advantage of my lack of importance at home. The man who caused me so much emotional and physical damage, that I live with the consequences decades later.

So, my birth name. A name with no originality, no individuality. A name that is a constant reminder of my past and of a family that failed me. Initials that mirrored my inability to bloom.

I am blooming now, though, like the lotus, that has roots in mud but blossoms into a beautiful flower when out of the water.

My family, no longer diminishing who I wanted to be, are in my past, and I now feel I have a future.

If I were a balloon, my name is the last string that tethers me to them; I am ready to cut that string.

I now feel I have a life; a life I can lead how I choose to, and that is what my chosen name indicates:

Vie, the French for life, is permanently tattooed on to my wrist as a reminder that I deserve to be here; that I have a life, and that, now, it is a good one.

My full name, now a representation of who I am: Vie Isabella Portland; la vie est belle; a true VIP.

Chapter Twenty

A lifelong romance

"To love oneself is the beginning of a lifelong romance." —
Oscar Wilde

If you had said to me, in my first three and a half decades, that I would feel the way I do about myself, that I am in a loving, equal, relationship, that I would have done the things I have, that I would be running my own multi-award winning business, I would have thought you were just being incredibly kind and, perhaps, a little bit patronising.

Who I am now is not someone I thought I could ever be. How could someone as fat, ugly and worthless as me achieve anything?

When I hit my lowest point, I knew I had three options: keep things the same; end things; change things. I, obviously, chose to change things. Now, this bit may be a little "crazy cat lady" for some of you, but I chose to stay because of my kitten, whom I mentioned at the beginning of the book; when I took her on, I promised her I would look after her for all of her life, and I knew no one would love her as much as I did. So I chose to stay for her; she is the reason I am alive. When she died in June 2020, I was utterly devastated; however, she lives on in my children's books.

My furry girl gave me a reason to stay, and I knew things couldn't stay the same, so the next thing was to decide how I was going to change things. There's a stumper for you!

I used to avoid mirrors, hating what I saw; if there was a reason to look in one, I would do it bit by bit, first my eyes, then my cheeks, rather than confront myself with the whole view; if I was looking at my clothes, I would look at top, then middle, then bottom; never the whole of me.

Now, mirrors don't scare me. Now, I can look in a mirror and be happy with what I see; even when I see a tired, or grey, looking me staring back. I no longer feel the need to criticise, but, instead, I show myself some compassion. If one of my conditions is having a flare, of course I look tired and drained, and I need kindness, not cruelty.

In the process of becoming who I am, one of the things I did was challenge myself with mirrors. Sometimes, I would look at my face, and tell myself I had to find things I liked; other times, I would say affirmations to my reflection.

Goodness! That felt awkward! At the beginning, I would often think about the character in the scary film (I don't do scary, so I've never seen the film, but it's not *Beetlejuice*) where, if you said their name three times, they appeared; I wondered whether by saying complimentary things about myself, some evil being, who hated boastful people, was going to appear and beat me to death with the mirror. Thankfully, I talked myself round from that quite quickly.

When I looked in a full length mirror, when my first thoughts were always derogatory, I would challenge myself to find the good. What did I see that I could possibly like? At first, it was things like, I like the way that my waist goes in; I like that I don't have varicose veins (if/when that happens as I get older, I will learn to accept those, too). I would focus on things my body could do. I would say thank you to my arms for allowing me to cuddle my cats. I would thank my feet for allowing me to dance, even though they hurt. Sometimes, it would be quite random, such as I would thank my boobs for allowing me to tassel twirl (it's far harder than it looks!), but the challenge was always to find something good, and I did. I built it up to liking how I look, to liking the way I dress, appreciating all the amazing things my body does.

I would also write comments on Post-it notes, lovely things people had said, and leave them on the mirrors; so they were always there as a reminder: I may not have liked what I saw, but others were complimentary about it. I made the decision to believe that others believed what they said when they said good things about me, even if the thought of believing them myself seemed ridiculous.

Even now, I still put stickers on the bathroom mirror. They currently read: "The world is wonderful and so are you" and "You are beautiful".

Something else that helped me was that I would write lovely things people said to me in a beautiful notebook: "My name is Vie and I have a glorious stationery habit!" Again, at first, I didn't believe them, but I believed that the person telling me did. I would write them in and read them whenever I was struggling. As time went on, I didn't always need to read the messages; just looking at the notebook, knowing what was written inside, gave me a boost.

With so many things now being online or via text/Whatsapp. I now screenshot lovely things people say, and I save them in a secret photo album on Facebook, that I've titled, "Lovely things people say".

Before I continue, I will say these things took time. They didn't happen overnight, and there were many times when I slipped out of the habit of doing it. The important thing is, though, that I started it back up. I would remind myself to do these things because I knew they made me feel better.

Maybe you're reading this and thinking, if it made you feel good, why did you stop doing it sometimes? The answer is that our minds are very powerful, and they can convince us of both wonderful and horrible things. I had to learn to challenge those thoughts, which was hard; living with consistent negative thoughts for so long was hard to overcome. It was my default, and, as distressing as it was, I knew how to live miserably. Sometimes, it's easier to choose what we know, even when it's hurtful, than challenge ourselves to be, to think, differently. It helped me to remind myself that my thoughts aren't facts; just because I think it, it doesn't mean it's true.

As part of beginning to accept who I am and what I look like, I believed I had to accept every aspect of me, even the bits that were, by the majority of people's standards, not pleasant.

Like many people, I used to hate using public toilets unless I really had to. If I had to, I would go for a wee but never anything more; I would rather suffer with tummy pain and discomfort than use a public toilet for anything more than a wee.

Then, my mental health plummeted. I rarely went out so, when I did, it was anxiety inducing. Unfortunately, for me, and probably many others, my bowels, oh so delightfully, responded to anxiety with gurgling and a strong desire to explode. I would be mortified that I had to run to wherever the closest washroom was and that my body would betray me with its own personal fanfare.

So embarrassing!!

Then the thought came to me that if I ignored those gurgly feelings, the possibilities of what could happen were even more humiliating! At the time I felt that to have a toileting accident, as an adult, in a busy shopping centre would be far beyond horrible. It was definitely better that I used the public toilets and that I just had to accept that my body was doing what it needed to. I also reminded myself that I had been brave enough to leave my little flat, and that definitely was a good step forward.

In my work with women, and in my personal life, I have met many women who are ashamed if their body makes a noise when they're using the loo; they are appalled that other people can hear what they're doing. I get it; I was the same. Then I realised what toilets are for: they are for us to get rid of whatever our bodies don't need, by whatever means necessary, and that we all need to use them. WE. ALL. NEED. TO USE. THEM. Every single one of us has made embarrassing stomach and bottom noises, but as it's our body just doing what it needs to do, it's best just to accept it. That's true body acceptance: acceptance for all that my body needs to do.

I'm not saying to go out, farting and burping loudly and indiscriminately; I am saying, when you are using a public toilet, and your own toilet at home, accept your body is just doing what it needs to do. Perhaps, if you, the reader, starts doing this (if you don't already), other people will follow your example. By being ourselves, we give others permission to be themselves, too. This is relevant to so much of what I say in this book.

Another part of me accepting the so far socially unacceptable things was understanding that my body needs to sweat more than most.

I mention in chapter 16, 'Courage and strength', one of the joyful side effects of my skin condition, EB, for me, is that I sweat easily.

For most of my life I hated that I sweated so much. I would feel dirty, smelly, and unfit (even though none of those things were true). I thought that it was another way for my body to torture me. I thought it was another way that demonstrated my body, that I, did not deserve to feel attractive.

As my confidence grew in other areas, I began to address this issue. And, again, I realised that it was just my body doing what it needed to do to keep me well. It's very clever, when you think about it.

For me, my two main triggers for blisters and shearing on my body are heat and friction. If I get too hot (which is not hot by many people's standards but is for my EB skin), I blister. The purpose of sweating is to keep our bodies at a good temperature.

When I sweat, my body is working really hard to cool me down to prevent me from blistering. It doesn't always work, but I really appreciate the effort. Thank you, body.

I also blister in my mouth and throat, mostly due to particular foods and, sometimes, drinks. When they are blistered, my mouth produces extra saliva, possibly because a dry mouth is more painful, and the blisters like to be moist (apologies if you are one of the many people who dislike that word). Extra saliva sometimes means I dribble. Although it's not to the extent of Homer Simpson eating donuts dribbling, I am very aware of it. When it happens, I explain to the people I am with, if it's the first time it's happened with them, why it's happening. For me to have gotten to this stage of acceptance, I had to tell myself that if anyone had a problem with it, it was theirs and not mine, and that, if they couldn't accept it, they weren't my people. Once I have explained it, no one has had a problem with it; most of them hadn't even noticed until I pointed it out. Again, it's just my body doing what it needs to.

While I am on the subject of embarrassing things, I thought I would cover a couple of others.

Life can trip us up in the silliest of ways. At the time, we usually want to run away and hide, hoping no one has seen our ineptitude, believing that even those on the other side of the planet witnessed it somehow.

Before I liked who I was, I got embarrassed A LOT. If I stumbled over a word. If I was asked to speak in class. If I got a question wrong. If anyone looked at me. As puberty hit, and my boobs blossomed, I was frequently the topic of conversation; I was one of the tallest in the class and then I had big boobs (in comparison to other students) to draw even more attention. I tried to hide. I wore baggier clothes and covered my face with my hair as much as possible.

On the rare occasion where I tried to embrace having such an adult figure, something would usually happen.

I was a teenager in the 80s; as a family, we were going to a party, and I had a new ra-ra dress (remember those?); this one was black with flowers, and it was strapless. My mum, after many derogatory comments about the "size of you", decided to sew thin straps on to the dress, because she said my boobs were so big, they would knock someone out if they weren't held in.

At this party were other families; in one family was a handsome older man (well, to me he was older; he was at least 17!). All the adults were drunk so I thought they wouldn't notice me doing anything, and, very sadly, I would sometimes seek out situations where I was likely to be rejected to confirm all the negative things I believed. This boy was sat with his brother; I decided to be brave and talk to him (we knew mutual people so I was just going to talk about them). I walked over to him; it was loud, and he couldn't hear me, so I bent over to get closer to his ear; the straps on my dress broke and my left boob fell out and hit him in the face. Awkward!!

At the time, I was desperate to get away. I refused to go to any parties where he might be from then on. I felt I had made a huge spectacle of myself, and I felt awful.

As the years have passed, though, it has become a story of amusement, one that very few people remember. I could even say it was probably the first boob he felt, so he possibly remembers it as a much more pleasurable experience than the one I had. And they didn't knock him out, despite what my mother warned.

Perspective matters.

And perspective helps when other potentially embarrassing things happen, too.

In the last few weeks, I have had two incidents happen that, had they happened before I had any confidence, I would have cried at the embarrassment, but, because I do, I just found them funny.

The first one was when I went into a coffee shop. A kind lady working there discretely told me that my dress had ridden up and I was flashing quite a lot of my legs; as I had been walking around, my shoulder bag had stuck to my dress and, step by step, pulled my dress further up; so it had probably happened before I even got close to the cafe. The lady was gentle with me, expecting embarrassment, but I smiled, thanked her, and said, "It's okay; I'm wearing knickers."

People that saw me saw a lot less of me than if I was on a beach in a bikini, but, because there was a potential risk of flashing my pants, there's a perceived element of embarrassment.

The next time was in my local coffee shop. There's quite the wind tunnel around it so, even on the sunniest of days, it can be a bit breezy. I pulled open the heavy door to go in and, as I stepped in, it slammed shut behind me, knocking me off balance so I stumbled in. Before, I would have been tempted to go home, or at least hide in a corner, assuming everyone had seen me make a fool of myself, but now, I just thought it was funny. I didn't do anything wrong; it wasn't my fault; there was no reason for me to feel like an idiot.

Perspective.

Often, people will say, "fake it 'til you make it". Although it's not as good as having true confidence, it certainly worked for me for a very long time.

I felt everything I did was an embarrassment, to me, and to everyone else. I felt I couldn't do anything right. When I started performing, for a very long time, I was convinced that I was going to be awful and that people would laugh at me because I was ridiculous, and not because I was doing comedy burlesque.

Oh! I should tell you how I got into burlesque!

I love musicals. One of my favourites is *Singing in the Rain* (Gene Kelly: swoon!). One day, I was watching it and, during the hoofer scene, where he sings *Gotta Dance*, the word "BURLESQUE" flashed up in a neon light. I pondered if anyone still did it, expecting it to be something that finished in the 1950s, so I Googled it; not only were people still doing it, but there was also a class starting very near where I lived!

Before I could convince myself otherwise, I booked on to the course and arranged a lift with a lovely lady who became a great friend.

I loved it! I was good at it! That was a very happy surprise.

One woman there, who was already a performer, wanted to put on a show and asked me to help; you'll probably know by now that I like to help, so, of course, I said yes.

She said I would have to perform. Oh no! Never!

In true panto style, we went back and forth: oh yes you will, oh no I won't.

I obviously did eventually agree to a one off performance and, well, you're reading this book, so you know the rest.

Anyway, every time, from the very first performance to the last, people would tell me how good I was. In the beginning, I thought people were being kind, but not honest. Yet, I did know that by getting on stage each time, I was demonstrating great courage, and that maybe, just maybe, the audience saw that in me but didn't want to say those words. And I really wanted to believe I was good. So I started faking that I felt it, that I felt I was a good performer, that people were telling me the truth.

Very soon after my first appearance, I got a message saying that a wonderful cabaret artist, who had become a friend, wanted me for their show. Their show was one of the biggest in the country with only the best performers from all over the world. Again, I thought they were just being nice, and it would never happen. But they weren't. Well, they were being nice, but they also believed in me. And it did happen. They booked me!

It was terrifying! And incredible!

It was in a large Victorian theatre, and we each had our own dressing rooms; how fancy is that!

And they paid me! My first paid gig!

I went on to perform at that show several times, but it was that first show that was the most special. Firstly, because it was wonderful to have someone who believed in me so much. Secondly, and, more importantly, because the money I got paid was the money I used to change my name.

Four days after performing, I officially became a VIP.

I was on a high for days! Both from the show and the name change. I had lots of messages with people telling me how good I was; how funny; how I was their favourite; how I gave them hope that they could be sexy at a higher weight, too.

WOW!!!

It was wonderful! And, after nearly every show, I had similar responses.

It was quite bizarre. There I was, someone who had always hated being the centre of attention, someone who had always hated their body, not only performing on a stage but also taking my clothes off, and people were loving it! They were loving me! It really helped me stop faking it and actually start believing it: I was good; I was attractive; I had talent.

Now, some of you reading this might think this was an extreme way of getting confidence (you're probably right) because you would never be naked in front of strangers. Again, perspective matters.

I was on a stage; I was taking my clothes off; I was stripping.

Now, have a think about when you go to the beach.

Do you sit there in all of your clothes? Or do you take them off, so that you are in your swimming costume or bikini?

It's probably unlikely that you get cheers and claps as you take your clothes off, but you are still stripping your clothes away.

And you'll be wearing far less than I ever did on stage. Every act I created, I would wear two pairs of large pants (safety pants and show pants); two pairs of tights, or one pair of tights under stockings; an underbust corset (on hot days I sometimes chose not to wear one); and pasties or tassels that were the size of side plates. Really, all people saw of my "naked" self was my arms, shoulders, and the outer areas of my boobs. Ooooooh. Sexy.

But context matters.

Although, logically, I was wearing far more than most people ever do on a beach, or at a pool, because I was taking my clothes off to music, with an audience, I was a stripper. On occasion, I was even called a sex worker, because I was titillating an audience. I never had a problem with that "insult" because I have no issue with sex workers, as long as they are working because they want to.

Burlesque was a huge part of me growing in confidence. Which is quite astounding. I had gone from being a girl, a woman, who hated being looked at, to willingly standing on a stage, performing in front of others.

There were a few exceptions to not wanting to be looked at before my burlesque career.

We went to several schools, as my father liked to buy derelict houses and do them up around us, so we moved a lot, and, in one of those schools, pupils were asked if they wanted to perform in assemblies. I never offered, but I was asked to dance sometimes. I usually danced with someone else.

The time I remember most clearly was a routine to Dollar's "Mirror Mirror"; the friend and I thought we were ever so clever, doing a routine where we mirrored each other's movements. I can picture myself so clearly; I was wearing a green and black striped skirt that had braces attached; a black roll neck top; thick black tights. I felt so grown-up; so worldly. I was 11 years old. And I had already been being raped for nearly three years. When I hear the song on the radio, my heart hurts for that little girl, and I really wish I could go back, as I am now to hug her and tell her that life will get better.

Another aside. Hugging.

A few months ago, we were watching a drama set during World War Two. One of the characters hugged someone, and I thought, "I didn't think hugging was invented then". A stupid thought, really, as hugging has probably been around for as long as we have. But, then I realised, for me, until I was an adult, hugging was not something I had in my life. I didn't realise it was a thing until friends started hugging me after I left home.

As positive as I am now, there will always be sadnesses, reminders of things never had.

Back to body acceptance.

Like many people, I have looked back at photos of a younger me and wished I was as fat as I thought I was then. It's sad that I spent so much of my time hating the body I had, even when it was healthier and smaller than I will ever be again.

But bodies change.

As children, our bodies tend to grow out, then up, time and again. As teens, hair grows in new places, and our bodies become shapes they've not been before. As adults, due to hormones, stress, pregnancy, menopause, exercise, illness, etc., our bodies get rounder, harder, softer.

And that's all normal. Yet we often feel we have to do everything to get our bodies back to a perceived ideal, even if it makes us unhappy, or ill.

Wouldn't it be wonderful if we all just accepted our bodies, and other people's bodies, just as they are? To not judge them on their shape, or size, or weight. Before anyone jumps in with, "But I am concerned about the pressure they are putting on their bodies/ the pressure on medical services, etc.", I urge you to read Lindo Bacon's work, and follow The Fat Doctor on Instagram. I will put the resources in the back of the book.

I know I am making this sound far easier than it is. And I will admit that there are times, though they happen rarely, when I begin to criticise my size.

Over the global crisis of Covid, like millions of others, I have borrowed* some weight; I would like to release/remove* it because some of my clothes don't fit (I love my clothes!). But, when I start to criticise, I remind myself of other things, such as, I have survived a global pandemic!!! That's the most important thing, not whether my arse is a size bigger! I can look down at my body, seeing the curves and mounds, and I see the Venus of Willendorf. I could find fault with the fat, but instead, I choose to remind myself that she is a representation of a goddess, which means I look like a goddess. I'm happy with that!

You may have noticed the * after *borrowed* and *release/remove*. Language is important, as I mention elsewhere in the book. When we talk about weight, we often say we have gained weight or that we want to lose weight; think about the words "gain" and "lose" in other contexts.

When we gain something, it's an object or goal we want to achieve; or it's an increase in wealth or resources. Our brains see it as a positive. If we have gained weight, maybe they'll see that as a positive, too, but by borrowing it, the plan is to only keep it temporarily.

And what do we want to do when we lose something? We usually want to find it.

This may not have any impact on your body size, but I hope that, at least, it will help you think about the language you use for everything you say to yourself, and others.

Chapter Twenty–One

Who I am

"The voice I finally heard that day was my own – the girl I'd locked away at ten years old, the girl I was before the world told me who to be – and she said: Here I am. I'm taking over now."
— *Glennon Doyle, Untamed*

In the years since I developed my confidence, I have been a part of so many wonderful things!

From performing burlesque, I started teaching it, and, very soon after, I started teaching vintage dance forms, too.

When I was at high school, the careers teacher would often encourage me to consider teaching as my future. I thought that was an impossibility. I didn't feel I was clever enough, and I certainly didn't think anyone would ever listen to me as the expert on any subject.

When I moved back to my birth city, I got a job in a high school as a Learning Support Assistant. As well as assisting in classrooms, I ran programmes to help the young people with their reading and others to help the dyslexic children. I could see I was getting results, and I knew the young people enjoyed their sessions with me because they told me so. They frequently asked if they could have more sessions with me, as they felt they were understanding more because of them. But I attributed the success to the fact they were just getting time with someone who could listen and who could take the time to explain things; it had nothing to do with me.

I didn't really understand the importance of being listened to because I hadn't ever been in a situation where I was allowed to share what I was feeling, at least, not ones where there was a positive outcome. The times I was brave enough to share my feelings at home, I was usually called something horrible and sent to my room. A couple of times I shared with friends about the awful things happening in my family, and they stopped being my friend. I learned to not share.

Now, I do understand. I firmly believe in being who I needed, and I am aware that I do that now, but pre-Vie, I didn't know. I just knew I didn't want any child to ever feel as stupid, as worthless, as unloved, as I did.

It started with my work with children, as a nanny, and carried through to my dance classes with adults.

I really love to dance, and it's something that has always been a part of my life, from dancing in my bedroom alone as a child, to dancing in the kitchen with the children I looked after, to teaching. It makes me happy. It brings me joy.

I've never been properly trained. My parents refused to pay for me to go to lessons, so my first ones were when I got a Saturday job in a newsagents and I could pay for myself. I was much older than everyone else in the class, so I learned the routines faster and would then help teach them. I didn't like that they would cry when they didn't understand what the teacher said, so I explained things in a simpler, often sillier, way.

And that's how I teach.

I have always welcomed everyone to my classes, especially those who say they can't dance. I want people to just feel joy in moving. At the beginning of every new class, I would say that there were no wrong moves, only unintentional solos, and that the best move on a dancefloor is always a smile. I wanted to remove the pressure of having to be "good". I wanted them to have fun.

I don't even use proper dance terms. A kick ball change became a "miniature pony, miniature pony"; a cross-legged spin became "need a wee"; salsa wiggles were taught by encouraging people to imagine their bottom cheeks were chewing toffee.

It's unlikely anyone in my classes was going to become the next Darcy Bussell, but they definitely had fun.

And so did I.

It was the same with the burlesque classes. I never asked anyone to do something I wasn't willing to do first. I would be honest about moves I found difficult and expressed that I had no issue with anyone being better than me at them (taking stockings off elegantly, pulling them over my head, while laying on my stomach, I'm definitely more donkey than Dita then!).

The best thing, though, was watching them all blossom.

Nearly all of them would come in, feeling awkward, believing they couldn't dance, believing they couldn't possibly be sexy, [1] and all of them would leave with a wiggle and some attitude. Brilliant! The day after a workshop (I prefer teaching burlesque as four or five hour workshops, rather than weekly classes), I would get messages telling me that they had been using one of the walks I had taught them on the way to drop the children off on the school run and that more people had smiled at them. One time, one of the ladies, who has become a much loved friend, went to her bank to ask for an overdraft and the bank manager also asked her out for dinner!

From doing my classes, some women got the confidence to change jobs, apply for promotions, move home, take up hobbies they thought they shouldn't do any more, and some even went on to perform.

There were even stronger results from my confidence workshops, which is marvellous!

In those workshops, there would be tears as people shared their stories, as they realised how many of us have similar ones, and because they had been holding them in so long. For those of us used to holding in our feelings, tears can be incredibly helpful. Without water, flowers don't bloom, and neither do we; tears are us watering our souls.

I would say the workshops were for body confidence, but really they were all-encompassing. So many of our body issues become the focus, hiding much deeper rooted ones. Some women were desperate to be smaller because they had been told they "took up too much space"; their opinions, their voices, were criticised and they were told they were too big. They didn't need to get smaller; they needed to believe they were worth being heard. Some women were told they were "too much", but they weren't. The people around them weren't enough, and it was easier for them to complain than change.

It didn't matter what size they were, as so many of their concerns were similar. We are taught to hold this shame inside of us, embarrassed to admit our insecurities, scared to share our perceived failures, feeling we're all alone in these worries, but, really, we all have so much in common.

The purpose of the workshops was to have the participants leave with tools to move on with their lives, with ways to challenge the negative thoughts, and tips to live happier, kinder, more confident lives. I wanted them to do what I had done: I wanted them to become their own friend.

I knew that my insecurities started in childhood, and through the burlesque and confidence workshops, it became apparent that I was not alone in that. Nearly every woman I taught said the same. Some would say that they wished they'd had someone like me in their lives when they were at school.

Periods

A little after I started the confidence workshops, I heard about a great community project, The Red Box Project, that wanted to help eradicate period poverty in schools. My periods have always been heavy, and there were many times when I bled through my school skirt, and because I didn't have enough period products with me, I would have to go to the school nurse, where I would be given a thick, looped towel to wear; it was very uncomfortable. The project resonated with me. I volunteered to run a branch.

I would take big red boxes (the clue was in the name) of period products into schools and colleges. I really enjoyed the conversations with the children and young people. Some were very knowledgeable, others had no clue, but it was great to have honest, open conversations with them about periods. It will come as no surprise, I'm sure, that I think open conversations are really important for us all to have, whether it be about our bodies, our health, or our emotions. It's not easy, but it's paramount to better relationships.

I loved being part of the project; I would give talks about periods to Brownies and Guides, and talks about period poverty at events; and the community really supported it. We don't have a big house, but we lost one whole room to the project as it was filled with period products (note: I say period products, rather than sanitary wear, since the project recommended it, and I fully agree with them. Those of us who have periods are not unsanitary; and the term *period products* does what it says on the tin/packet).

I really loved it but, after two years of running that, and almost a year before being involved with Pride (I must tell you about that!), I needed to stop and focus on what I wanted to do for my dreams, for my business. As it happened, within three months of me passing my branch to someone else, the project started to wind down in my area as the government had said they would start ensuring that products were provided to schools.

Pride!

In June 2016, there was a horrific incident in Orlando, Florida, where a man killed 49 people, and wounded 53 others, in a gay nightclub. I have many LGBTQ+ friends, and the thought of them being victims of such hatred filled me with dread, and I wanted to do something.

I put a post on Facebook and asked why the city I am in, as one of the biggest cities in the UK, didn't have a Pride event. Nobody really knew why but several people said, "Why don't you do it, Vie?" There's a quote, by Lily Tomlin, "I always wondered why somebody doesn't do something about that. Then I realized I was somebody."

Well, it looked like I was that somebody.

I wanted to create an event that represented the world I want to live in; I wanted it to be an environment where people could walk hand in hand with who they loved, with no judgement, no hatred, just more love.

I had lots of conversations with lots of local people and they were fully behind it. Then I found out that the owner of a local bar/theatre and one of her staff members wanted to set up a Pride too, so we decided to organise one together. Just like that.

Within the next ten weeks, we attended so many meetings, some on things we hadn't known you had to have meetings about! We put on fundraising events; we schmoozed with sponsors; we organised volunteers; and we built up huge excitement.

I did receive the occasional comment. A few people asked why I was bothering when I don't present as LGBTQ+ — what do they know?! I have always been of the thought that it's the person that matters, not the bits between their legs! One person sent me a sickly sweet message saying that, now I had started it, perhaps I should leave and let the people who really knew what they were talking about to do it. I asked LGBTQ+ friends what they thought

— without exception, they were fully behind me and said that if that person thought they were the right person for the job, why hadn't they done it before?! Exactly!!

On the day, we were expecting around 500 people; we thought that would be a great number for a first event. Over 5000 people came! It was incredible! Most of the time, I wasn't aware of just how many people were there, as I was so busy, either on a stand, or running around checking on people, but, one time, I went up to a room in the bar and could see all the way along the street: WHOAH!!! That was a lot of people! I had a wave of panic, wondering how we were going to keep all of those people happy, and then I reminded myself that the best thing I could do was get down there and do the best I could.

It was a wonderful event. One of my favourite things of the day was when I was approached by a boy, around 6 to 8 years old; he offered me a donut from a big box from the local supermarket. I said it was very kind of him, and he explained that he was really enjoying the event because all he could see was love, and he wanted to return that love the best way he knew how: by giving people donuts. My heart!

It was a long, exhausting day, and I am so proud of the whole event.

I threw myself into the event, before and after, and I planned to be around for a long while, but, sadly, I frequently disagreed with the committee's views on the events and other things and, as I am very much about finding your own happiness, I chose to leave. I will admit that I sometimes get sad when I see each year's photos crop up, but then I remind myself that the sadness is very brief in comparison to all the hard work and the frustrations I felt. I don't regret leaving.

And now, I get to be involved with other local LGBTQ+ events that are far more in line with who I am, as they are far more inclusive and community based.

Finding my focus

Now, my main focus is my own community project. After being heavily involved in two other community projects, and helping occasionally with others, the time came to focus on mine.

For me, it seemed that my entire life, all my experiences, have come to this point, wrapped in a big box with a bow, and presented me with the idea I had for my Community Interest Company.

For those of you who don't know, I have a Community Interest Company that teaches self-esteem and confidence to children, young people, and women. I work with children as young as 4, as that's when school starts in the UK, and it's from the age of 3 that children start making judgements about their own and others' bodies, to young people of 19, in schools, colleges, and groups. I work with women one to one, as well as in domestic refuges, crisis centres, and other groups.

I love what I do! I am incredibly grateful that I have the skills and knowledge to do it, and I feel it's a privilege to spend time with all of these people as they blossom.

What I do in classes of four-year-olds is, obviously, very different to what I do in a class of 15-year-olds. With primary school groups I read stories, do simple activities, and we chat. And giggle. The giggling is fun.

With the slightly older primary groups, aged seven and up, I play a game that was designed to question perceptions of how people look. One question is to ask them if they can think of someone who looks like they're going to be a baddie but they're actually good; Shrek is a good example. It's not surprising that we all have impressions of how the evil-doer is going to look; have a think about the villains in films and on tv — many of them are fat, bald, disabled, or disfigured. The message is difference = bad.

Sometimes, teaching staff will come in and give me information about particular pupils; even the most well-meaning of people can be heavily biased. At the beginning of one session, a staff member said, "She won't talk because she thinks she talks funny." She didn't "talk funny"; she had an accent. During the session, this little girl opened up and talked about how she had travelled from one country and lived in two others, before arriving in the UK; she spoke a good level of several languages! Amazing! Before they left the classroom, the other pupils were asking her to say rude words, like "bum", in different languages. It was beautiful to witness; she now felt able to use her voice.

Another time, I was told "Not to bother" with one girl because she had ADHD and I wouldn't get anything out of her. At the beginning of the session, she lived up to the staff member's expectations and she became very troubled by a fly; as it buzzed around, she flapped, she screamed, and she chased. As the rest of the group discussed a question I had asked, I went to her and asked if she knew what the fly was thinking; she said no; she said it was loud; I said that perhaps the fly was lonely; that maybe it was loud and buzzing closely at people because it wanted their attention, as they had no friends. She was still. Then she said she would be the fly's friend. The rest of the session she sat, very quietly, chatting to the fly.

With high school students and youth groups it depends on what I am asked for. It could be conversation based, with me asking questions and then following their lead (it's important they feel they have control over some of the topics, because it's important they feel heard). Sometimes, it will be about helping them realise their strengths. Other times, I will get them to loudly shout positive affirmations. I have an plethora of tools for each age group.

One thing I always do with the high school students is get them to write a compliment on a Post-it note to everyone on their table; well, that's how it starts. Usually, by the last sessions of the day, word has got out — "Miss, are you the one that makes us say nice things and be loud?" "Yes, that is me." — and they want to do them for everyone in the class, which is wonderful!

It's a great tool to help each other see that people usually see us in a far more complimentary light than we see ourselves.

Although, one time, I worried it had gone horribly wrong.

I was with a group of 14/15 year old girls. It was evident that there had been a falling out, as one of a group sat on a separate table with two young people she didn't appear to know well. This young woman, and all her usual friends, were heavily made up, immaculately dressed, and they seemed to be the group to follow. But, for this session, shooting furtive glances at her friends, she sat with two others.

I asked them all to write something lovely about everyone on their table. They all put their heads down and started writing.

I looked at the girl who had separated herself and her bottom lip was quivering. I worried this was the time it had gone wrong and that the girls she was with had said something upsetting.

I went over to her and crouched by her side, asking if everything was okay.

She held out the Post-it note; it said: You are so beautiful!

She said, "I've never been called beautiful before."

I asked her how she felt, and, through her tears, she said, "beautiful" with a smile.

Frequently, I have to hold back tears in my work (I don't always manage to), and this was one of those times. It was such an honour to witness that! I love my job!!

With women, there will be questions, discussions, sometimes a film. Again, it's important that they feel they can ask questions, that they can guide where the session goes. I hear so many heart-breaking things, but it's wonderful when the women start to realise how incredible they are and how they can make the changes they need to be happier.

Throughout a lot of my life, family and partners would say I was bragging if ever I said anything good about myself; it was an insult. They were telling me I had no reason to feel proud. Now, those people are no longer in my life, and I know I have many reasons to be very proud of myself. I also think that we should all be happy to share who we are and what we're good at; some may see it as bragging; others will see it as a celebration of who we are.

And, for myself particularly, if I don't feel confident saying that I am good at my chosen job, well, I wouldn't be a great example of being a confidence coach, would I?!

And I am good at my job.

I have my degree, and I have done counselling qualifications, so I have the academic knowledge, as well as all of the many books I have read. But, I feel, it's my life experiences that matter far more.

Growing up feeling unloved, I can empathise with others who feel the same, and not dismiss how they feel.

Growing up in an abusive environment, I have gentleness and understanding beyond textbooks. And I know the power of words, how they can hurt.

Living in a relationship with domestic abuse, I remember how it feels to not be able to "just leave", to believe all that is said, to be too scared to leave.

Being someone who lived with low self-esteem and no confidence, I understand how it pervades your very being, how everything can feel "too much", as if confidence is for other people, that "this" is all there is.

I know a lot about grief, as I have lost so much.

I know about inclusion because I have been excluded.

I'm good at what I do because I have lived it.

I'm good at lots of things because I have learned, and tried, and hoped.

I have taken one brave step after another, and I have changed my life for the better.

Now, do you want to take a brave step? Where will you start?

---

1. Sexy - I don't believe we should ever be expected to be sexy; I believe we should be who we want to be. And who determines what is sexy anyway?!

Chapter Twenty–Two

Beautiful wounds

"Our wounds are often the openings into the best and most beautiful parts of us." — David Richo

When I lost my job and was told I would never be well enough to work again, I knew I had to try something. It took me weeks, but I finally worked up the courage to contact the local Rape Crisis Centre. We arranged an appointment for me to go in and talk to them. They warned me that there was a long waiting list and that I wouldn't be seen for months. Although I had made the brave step to contact them, I wasn't sure I was ready to talk about everything, so I was happy to wait.

I was so anxious! I was convinced they would tell me that what I had been through wasn't that bad; that I was obviously pathetic for still struggling all these years later.

I went to the appointment. I was asked to give my history and explain why I was there. I told the lovely woman I was speaking to about my parents, about the abuse, about the wider family, about why I was back in my birth city, about how much I was struggling. She didn't say much, but she gave lots of encouraging, sympathetic noises and nods of her head. At the end, she told me she thought I was amazing that I had survived so much. I thought she was just being kind.

Within a week they telephoned and booked me in quite quickly.

Apparently, I was such an interesting case, they wanted to start working with me sooner. It's quite disconcerting, being told that you're an interesting case by professionals; I've had psychiatrists and doctors say it to me, as well as the people at Rape Crisis. For me, then, it felt like I was being singled out as an oddity, a specimen to be studied, a freak.

However, now, I am so very grateful that I got seen so soon. I am also very grateful that I had over a year's worth of appointments before they then had to start limiting the number of appointments due to budget cuts.

I have had a lot of therapy in my adult years. Even now, I go for "top ups" every few years, because I know the value of talking to someone who doesn't know me, has no preconceived notions of me, who just allows me to talk, and they guide me to answers.

However, not all therapists are good. I urge you to trust your instincts, even if you feel that you can't be trusted with your decisions, because, if you feel bad talking to them, you won't get the best results.

The worst one I saw was when I was at university. My then partner, Tom, was telling me how rubbish I was at sex (he would also tell me how good I was; if you've read chapter 13, the contradiction will become more understandable) and that I had to go to a doctor. My doctor referred me to a psychosexual therapist.

Have you read or seen *Matilda*? (As an aside, Matilda is the character I relate most to in any story; interestingly, on seeing the stage show, I realised I had also become my own Miss Honey.) As soon as I saw this therapist, she reminded me of The Trunchbull; she was a tall, imposing, older woman (close to retirement), wearing a tweed two piece, and she didn't talk, she boomed!

At the first appointment, she roughly examined me to make sure everything was "working sufficiently" (her words). With the aggressive way she moved her fingers around inside of me, I felt rather like a pinball machine. She started spouting Freudian theories at me; I already knew I disliked Freud but, being the good girl I am, I listened and waited for something to agree with. The second time I went to see her, she told me that the reason I don't get on with my father is because he had never offered to have sex with me. As I said, I really, intensely, dislike Freudian theories. I was, however, grateful that I knew enough about Freud, and other schools of thought, to know that she was talking utter rubbish. I didn't go back.

So, if you don't feel comfortable with your therapist, leave!

When in therapy, be honest and open. As a coach, I can honestly reassure you that there is very little I haven't heard, and it takes a lot to surprise me; counsellors are the same. By being truthful, you are more likely to get what you need from them; you are there to change things, to feel better about things, and they can only help if you are genuine with them.

Chapter Twenty–Three

Fancy packaging

"It's who we are and what we do that matters; the rest is just fancy packaging." — Vie Portland

I wish I could tell you that learning to love who I was just happened overnight, but that would be a lie.

I'm also not going to tell you to do all the things I did, because the first two steps to me accepting myself were awful. I will tell you about those two things before I get on to the good stuff.

Before my EB was diagnosed, I didn't really know how to look after my blisters, so they frequently got infected. One Friday evening, I absent-mindedly scratched an infected blister, then scratched my lip. Within minutes, I was vomiting. I couldn't keep anything in for a whole week. I kept thinking to myself, "At least I will lose weight".

I didn't.

A couple of years later, I was really ill with tonsillitis but, because I had just started a new job, in a new area, I hadn't signed up with a new doctor's surgery, and, even if I had, taking time off in your first week wasn't great. So I kept going, getting more and more exhausted, and not being able to eat very much because my throat was extremely swollen.

On the Saturday morning, I gasped myself awake, feeling like I was struggling to breathe. I thumped myself in my chest a few times, as if that would help me kickstart my normal breathing pattern. I was panicking and I called NHS 111. The lady at the other end of the line told me to call an ambulance because I was close to dying.

As a further indicator of how little I felt of myself at the time, I told myself that I couldn't possibly call an ambulance as that would be a waste of the paramedics' time, and that there were far more important people who needed them that weren't me. So I got a taxi to the nearest A&E, expecting to be waiting a long time.

Triage saw me within a few minutes, and, within a few minutes of that, I was being wheeled to be seen urgently. I was in hospital for six days. I couldn't eat and the medication was making me vomit, because no one told me that the medication needed food, too.

There was a beautiful, older Pakistani lady in the bed opposite me; she spoke only a few words of English, so we communicated mostly through eye contact and weak smiles. However, whenever I started being sick, she would rush out of her bed to come to me, and stroke my back, saying "There, there". It was the only time anyone had ever done that to me, and it really felt like love. I really wish I had got her details because I would have loved to have sent her a heartfelt thank you.

Again, I kept telling myself that surely I would lose weight this time, having barely eaten for almost two weeks!

Nope.

I resigned myself to the fact that I would always be fat and ugly. So, I accepted that my body would always be the way it is, but I certainly wasn't happy with it.

Thankfully, several years later, I began the journey towards happiness.

Trying new things

I told you earlier in the book about how burlesque was a huge part of changing how I felt about myself. I highly recommend it as a way of helping you feel more confident; however, I also know it's not everyone's thing.

For me, the things about it that contributed to how I felt were that I risked trying something new. I learned new skills, and I learned I was good at something.

It can be really hard to try something new, especially if you don't feel you have for a very long time. It can feel scary and intimidating; worries of feeling or looking stupid are prevalent in our minds. We worry that others will think we're ridiculous for being there; we get concerned that everyone else there will know what they are doing and that there may as well be a neon sign above our heads, highlighting us and all the mistakes we are bound to make. We think others there will be judging us on how we look and noticing the size of our bums.

I remember the feelings so well!

But I'm going to tell you something: nearly everyone else there will be feeling much the same, and they won't be concerned about you because they're too worried about themselves. Some of the others who might not feel that way, will be kind and welcoming. And, if there is anyone that isn't either of those things, and they seem a bit Judgy McJudgeson, well, they're either masking the insecurities they feel, or they might quite possibly just be a knob, and they are not your people.

When I facilitate confidence workshops, whether for teenagers or women, I ask them to write on Post-it notes their first impressions of the other people in the room, and then either I hand them out or they put them on big bits of paper I have put on the wall. They're always anonymous.

There are always tears when the notes are read out.

It takes bravery to try something new, as I've said, and especially in a workshop where long held beliefs are going to be challenged, so emotions are frequently close to the surface. Everyone expects that, at worst, the comments will mirror their insecurities, that everyone did notice the size of their bum as they walked in, and, at best, that they like the top they're wearing.

But they aren't like that.

The notes say:

"You have a beautiful smile."

"Your eyes really shine."

"I love your whole style."

"You have a wonderful presence."

"I wish I looked like you."

You see, although there are some who will pick on your perceived flaws, usually because of their own insecurities, the majority of people, if they notice anyone at all because they're so worried about how they look, will see your beauty. They will see the things you have forgotten to look for. They see you.

So, whether you have always longed to learn synchronised swimming, quantum physics, or to join a book club that's all about dinosaurs, go! Join! Be brave! An adventure awaits!

Positive/negative jars

As you have seen through reading this book, I have had a lot of negative thoughts about myself; we all do. We all have that little bully that lies inside of us, waiting to jump on us every time we feel insecure. I'm not sure they ever fully go away, but you can certainly tame them.

When I had decided to start making changes, I knew that I had to stop believing so much of my negative self-talk. I set myself a challenge.

Every time I thought something negative about myself, I had to come up with two positives.

It was difficult for a long time. I had rarely complimented myself on anything ever, so this was going to be really difficult! But I had to try.

The negatives obviously came easily but, at first, finding the positives was a struggle.

My two positives in the beginning were things like:

- I said thank you to the lady in the shop (demonstrating I am polite).
- My girls (my cats) sat on my lap (showing that my girls think I am worth loving).
- I danced really energetically to that song in the kitchen (contradicting a negative about being lazy).
- Someone smiled at me kindly (this one was quite big for me; it meant someone noticed me; it meant I was worth smiling at; and it meant someone felt I deserved kindness).

As time went on, the positives got more personal:

- I am kind.
- I have a good sense of style.
- I am doing well at college (I was studying for my counselling qualifications at the time).
- People like how I dance.

And now, I happily tell myself how brilliant I am frequently, even when I am feeling low. There have been times during the Covid pandemic that I have had fleeting thoughts of giving up my business, fearing I couldn't make it work. Then I remind myself of how fantastic it is that I even set up a business in the first place

— that I have created products and written children's stories, proving how adaptable I am and how I am willing to learn new skills; that I've met new people and taken new opportunities; and I've done all of this while living with several disabilities! I'm a marvel!

Some people reading this may lean back and suck in breath at that last comment. As women, especially, we often feel we have to underplay what we are capable of; we are told not to brag; we're told not to be arrogant.

But why? Why shouldn't we celebrate our successes? We've worked hard for them!

Anyway, I digress. Though, I shall come back to it.

What I ask the people I work with to do is to have two jars. Every time they have a negative thought, they write it on a Post-it note (I should get shares in Post-it notes!) and put it in the negatives jar. Then, they have to come up with two positives, only writing one per piece of paper, and put both bits in the positives jar. And no cheating! It can't be the same two positives all the time! They have to find different ones. This is an exercise to help them see more of their positives.

If they do the exercise regularly, it soon becomes obvious that there are far more positives than negatives.

The next challenge is to start believing them. By saying those positives, either to ourselves in our head or out loud, our brain starts taking note, and, over time, those negative thoughts don't interfere as frequently.

And now, the next challenge!

Accepting compliments

How many times has someone paid you a compliment and you have dismissed it?

How many times have you said, "Don't, I look a mess."

Or, "Don't. I look so fat."

Or, "It's really cheap."

As a quick aside, when giving compliments, NEVER compliment on weight! "You look good, have you lost weight?" Why? Because, with that one sentence, you are implying that the person didn't look good before they lost weight. Also, you don't know whether the person has lost weight due to a health issue, or stress; or you may be another trigger to them thinking that they can only look good thinner and start a terrifying battle with an eating disorder. And our worth should never be tied up with numbers. A simple, "You look lovely!" is great!

Now, I want you to think about when you receive a gift.

Your great aunt Ermintrude has given you lily of the valley bath cubes for your birthday. You only have a shower. Do you yell at great aunt Ermintrude and tell her she is wrong? Do you throw her gift back at her? No; you smile sweetly, say thank you, quietly decide you'll give them to a charity shop, and move on.

Now, imagine every compliment as a gift.

Someone says to you, "You look beautiful" and you say, "Don't, I look a mess" — you are telling them that you believe they are wrong. You are telling them that you don't appreciate them taking time out of their day to say something lovely to you.

That person wants to tell you about something good they see in you (this does not apply to cat calls; they are intrusive and inconsiderate, and, frequently, offensive); you may not believe what they're saying but believe that they believe it.

See it as a gift and say, "Thank you."

The more practice you get at this, the more you will start believing what those around you are saying to you. You will start believing that you are as wonderful as they think you are.

Be proud!

As I've said earlier in this chapter, women often feel they can't share their accomplishments for fear of being accused of arrogance or of bragging. But why shouldn't those accomplishments be shared if you want to share them?

I'm not telling you that you hire a bus with your image and "Vera did good" plastered all over it, shouting from a Tannoy about all the brilliant things you've done (although, if that's what you want to do, you do it! And let me know so that I can celebrate with you!), but there's nothing wrong with telling those you want to share it with.

As you do this, see yourself as leading the way. For all those girls and women who came before you, too scared to share their accomplishments, you step forward and celebrate, and show others that it's great to be who we are.

You are a shining example of brilliance.

Chapter Twenty-Four

Out of business

"If tomorrow, women woke up and decided they really liked their bodies, just think how many industries would go out of business." — Dr Gail Dines

I use this quotation frequently in my work. Advertisements are trying to sell us things to make our face less wrinkled, our hair less grey, our dimpled bottoms less cellulite-y. The adverts want to make us feel that we aren't good enough, otherwise we wouldn't buy those products.

But what if we realised we are good enough, just as we are?

Too often, we think of our bodies in terms of numbers:

- How much it weighs.
- What dress size it is.
- How many calories it's taken in.
- How many calories it's burned.
- How many miles it can walk/run.
- How many reps it can lift at the gym.

And those numbers are rarely what we believe we should want them to be.

We live in a society that's drowning in diet culture. We're told how we're meant to look. We're told what we're meant to weigh.

We're told what type of body we are meant to have.

We're also fed negative messages if we don't fit those ideals. Those people living in larger bodies (and I am one of them) are told that they must eat too much, that they're greedy, that they're lazy, if they don't fit the ideal. Many medical conditions are ignored, with patients instead being told that if we lose weight, we'll be "fixed".

In her article, "Obesity is a Chronic Disease", Sarah Le Brocq states that, "In reality, obesity is a very complex disease; over one hundred factors can be contributing causes of obesity." For the majority of us, our weight is not higher because we only sit on the sofa, eating takeaways and huge bars of chocolate and bags of crisps; there are many other factors.

I mentioned elsewhere in the book about how advertisers are getting paid to make us feel that we aren't good enough so that we buy more products. To the serial dieters amongst you, take a deep breath because you may not like this part: the diet industry is a multi-billion dollar a year industry, and it stays that way by ensuring that the majority of diets fail, thus making you feel like a failure. It's really not you! Your body is doing the best it can!)

Think about it: if everyone did well on diets, would people need to keep renewing their WW/SW/Noom etc. membership? Surely, if it was as easy as they make it out to be, we would all only need to sign up once? But, no; every study done on the efficacy of diets for weight loss has shown they don't work for the majority of people, yet it's us, the ones paying out the money, the ones beating ourselves up because we don't meet an ideal, who are made to feel like failures.

Lindo Bacon's books are a great resource for learning more about how and why diets fail, as well as all the studies done (I will share resources later in the book). I am not a scientist, so I will urge you to look at their books instead. They are also the founder of the Health At Every Size programme.

However, I will share these paragraphs from Bacon's books about the incredibly flawed Body Mass Index (BMI) Scale:

Consider BMI, which we are taught to use as a basis for defining someone's health status. When the United States established the standards that it and many other countries currently use, the data the committee examined showed that health decrement didn't occur until there was a BMI of 40, although they set the standard for overweight at 25 and obesity at 30. When [Bacon] queried a committee member about why they set the numbers this way in the absence of supporting research, her response was that they got a lot of pressure to conform to international standards.Examine those international standards, set by the World Health Organisation (WHO), and you will find that the WHO relied on the International Obesity Task Force (IOTF) to make the recommendations. At the time, the two biggest funders of the IOTF were the pharmaceutical companies that had the only weight-loss drugs on the market. In other words, the pharmaceutical industry, which has a vested interest in making us believe that fat is dangerous — and that they have a solution — wrote the BMI standards that are currently used. (Bacon, L., *Body Respect*. 2014. Pages 14—15)

When I was at university, we were taught to always question studies; we were taught that it is always prudent to see where the money that paid for the study was coming from, because that's where the bias will lie. Always check the source of the money.

A little bit of what you fancy does you good.

Now, I know there will be some of you reading this who want to completely ignore the evidence available that diets mostly don't work. Many of you may be thinking that you could never be happy in the body you are in (please do try the things I have already suggested!); you may be feeling a sense of panic that this is the way you'll always be.

Breathe. I find in for four, out for six works well.

Before I liked who I am, my eating habits were awful. When I was a nanny, I would often munch my way through seven or eight cheap chocolate bars, eat the children's leftovers, then, when I got home, either have a ready meal or crisps and more chocolate because I was tired.

When my mental health was at its worst and I was living alone, I would often go days where I would just eat cereal and chocolate, unless it was in the couple of weeks after I had a frozen food delivery, and I would add frozen dinners to the menu.

I didn't care what I put in my body because I didn't care about my body.

I also wasn't aware of how much I used food in response to my emotions.

I felt miserable so I ate chocolate to cheer me up.

I felt tired so I would eat easily cooked processed food.

I felt lonely so I would eat whatever was close to hand.

I felt I didn't deserve to be nourished and cared for, so I didn't see myself as worthy of eating nutritious food.

I'm not saying I don't eat these things now, but things are different.

Now, if I feel I am reaching for food as a replacement for something else I need, I think about what I need instead. Before I would eat crisps and chocolate to mask the pain of sadness and loneliness; now, I don't need to mask it because I can deal with feeling it, and I will ask someone I care about to give me a hug or meet me for a chat. When I feel tired, I will reach for a banana or some cashew nuts.

Please don't see this as me saying to not eat the chocolate! I rarely drink alcohol (it's usually a Pimms or two a year); I've never smoked; I don't drink tea or coffee (well, I do like green and iced teas, and I can't drink coffee as I have a very bizarre reaction to it); so chocolate is my thing. But I only eat good quality chocolate. Before, I could easily eat seven bars a day; now a bar will last me two or three days.

Also, it's the way I eat it. Before, I would shovel it into my mouth, barely tasting it; now, I eat it slowly and I make sure I taste it, that I savour it.

Have a think about how and what you eat:

• Do you have a tendency to reach for a glass of wine when you've had a hard day?

• Do you start raiding the fridge for cheese when you're angry?

• Do you have a secret stash of chocolate for when you feel lonely?

Do you think about what you are feeling before you reach for these foods? Or is it an automatic action that you do without thinking?

Have a think about it. The next time you have a hard day, instead of reaching for the wine, ponder what made it a hard day, and make plans for how to make it better. You'll feel more in control, and, hopefully, happier, so if you still have a glass of wine, it won't be to drown your sorrows but to be enjoyed instead.

Before you start gnawing at the Cheddar, think about what made you angry. Why did it make you angry? How did it make you feel? What would you have liked to happen instead? How could it be different next time? If you still want the cheese, take your time eating it; savour the flavours, the smells; and relish feeling better about making changes.

Before you get the secret stash of chocolate out from wherever you keep it, think about why you feel lonely. Have you been missing seeing people? Someone in particular? Do you feel your emotional needs aren't being met? Now decide what can be changed. Arrange to see a friend for a catch up. Arrange a meal out or a picnic with a group of friends. Try something new to meet new friends.

When you learn to not self-medicate with food but deal with your emotions instead, food can become more pleasurable. We all need food to survive but enjoy it, too. Appreciate the way that good chocolate has a lovely crisp sound on breaking and a smooth sensation as it moves around your mouth; revel in the mango as its juices drip down your arm and its flavour explodes on your tongue; take pleasure in the smell of the cheese and its texture.

Try to not use food as a form of medication. And try not to use it as reward or punishment, either.

Enjoy food. Appreciate food.

As I write this, we're at the tail end of the global pandemic that is Covid. Many of us have felt isolated and lonely; many of us have captured a little weight. Please don't beat yourself up about it because your body has done something incredible! It has survived a pandemic; it has kept you alive; it has kept you going. Don't punish it, yourself, for doing something so wonderful. You have survived!

And that takes me on to the next bit.

Celebrate your body!

Many of us will look at our bodies and criticise them.

We look at each part of our body and say what we want to be different. We want it to be bigger or smaller; longer or shorter; smoother or rounder.

Instead of criticising, think about what it allows you to do.

My arms are big. Because I live in a larger body, I have bingo wings; because of my disabilities, sometimes having to support myself up and down stairs, I have biceps (incidentally, a few years ago, I contemplated writing a book, never thinking it would happen, but I wrote the chapter title: Biceps and Bingo Wings). I could disparage them, moan that it's difficult to find sleeves that cover my arms, but I don't because I really value them. Yes, they are big, but they do help me move sometimes, and I am grateful for that. They allow me to give hugs to people I care for and that's wonderful; they allow me to stroke my cats, which brings me great pleasure; they allow me to throw friends' children into the air, which we all love. My arms are brilliant.

My feet are scarred, and they are always sore. But they allow me to walk to meet my friends; they allow me to dance, which is one of my favourite things to do; they allow me to walk around my favourite places.

Think about your body.

Think how amazing it is to allow you to do so much.

Some of you reading this will have climbed mountains, learned to drive, or love to cook. You may be a marathon runner or an author; there are so many things that you do that you just wouldn't be able to do if you didn't have that magnificent body of yours.

Some of you reading this will have given birth. Many of the people I work with will bemoan how their once flat stomach is rounded, or how the scars are ugly. Now, think, would you swap your pre-pregnancy tummies for your child? The skin, the scars, are testament to how incredible your body is! You created a human! Wow!!

For someone like me, who would have loved to have a child but couldn't, I would happily take the scars for the joy of a child.

What I am going to ask you to do next will probably feel weird. At first, at least.

Thank your body.

From thanking your heart and lungs for keeping you going, to every extremity that allows you to do all the things you enjoy.

Thank everything for allowing you to be who you are.

And make this a regular practice. Do it when you are feeling good and especially do it when you are not, to remind yourself of how fantastic your body is. You can do it in front of a mirror, or you could set it as a routine, so every time you go to the kitchen to make a cup of tea, you thank all the bits of your body that are working to allow you to do that.

You may feel that you'll never get to a place of loving your body, so aim for acceptance.

And please don't ever beat yourself up about any of this. Try when you can and celebrate when you do.

For many of us, we have been living in bodies we are not happy in for a long time; it's not going to change overnight.

But I am proof that it is possible.

I hated my body for how it looked, for how damaged it was, for the things that it allowed others to do to me.

Now, I dress my body the way I want, and I feel good about it.

I am grateful that, despite everything that is broken or wonky in me, my body still allows me to do so many of the things I love.

And I am in awe that it has survived everything it has lived through.

My body is bloody brilliant! And so is yours.

Chapter Twenty–Five

Brave, strong, smart

"You're braver than you believe, and stronger than you seem, and smarter than you think." — Christopher Robin (A.A. Milne)

This chapter isn't just for parents; it's for everyone who ever comes in contact with a child, whether it's through work, family, or friends.

When I work with women, nearly all of them will express a deep insecurity about one, or more, parts of their body. When we think about the insecurity and where it comes from, a huge percentage (I can't actually think of anyone where what I am about to say isn't relevant, but there's always someone who will prove us wrong, so I shall stick with the huge percentage comment) can trace it back to a flippant comment from a parent, sibling, family member, teacher, friend.

"You can't eat any more of that; you will get fat."

"Look at those chubby thighs!"

"You have a round tummy!"

"Your nose is growing!" — in relation to a child telling a fib.

And, for me, it was my family telling me how fat and ugly I was.

As children, we're told to believe what grown-ups say, so, when a grown-up says these things to us, we believe them. Children can also think in absolutes; there might not be any wavering on the statement.

Goodness! The number of times a parent has contacted me saying that, after a "healthy eating" session at school, their child is now refusing to eat anything with sugar in it, or, if they do, they have to do several laps around their home to "get rid of it". I've even chatted to parents living in poverty whose children are really depressed because they feel a failure for not being able to afford to eat the "healthy food" their teacher talked about.

This is absolutely not about the teachers. I think teachers are brilliant and work really hard, often with little gratitude.

This is about the language we use.

And it's about understanding that our mental health is as important as our physical health; it's about understanding that life is to be lived and enjoyed and that nearly everything in moderation is good.

And it's about understanding that no matter what size, shape, race, gender, sexuality, or ability, no one deserves to be shamed because of who they are.

Here are some alternatives for you.

Instead of, "You can't eat any more of that; you will get fat." Say, "Let's save some of it for tomorrow so the enjoyment lasts for even longer!"

Instead of, "Look at those chubby thighs!" Say, "Your thighs are so strong!". Or don't say anything at all.

Instead of, "You have a round tummy!" Say, "Your tummy is wonderful!" Or, again, say nothing at all.

Instead of "Your nose is growing!", in relation to a child telling a fib, if it's about a game, for example, you are playing hide and seek and they are telling you someone is hiding somewhere other than where they are, say, "Are you pretending? You're very good at pretending!" If it's a fib about something more serious, sit with them and try to understand why they felt the need to not tell you the truth.

And the example I used about me, well, you are reading the book that tells you how I overcame that.

Studies

In the rest of this chapter I will share a few pieces of research to highlight that these issues are, sadly, common place, before going on to share things people can do to have happier, more confident children.

Children as young as three have body image issues and some four-year-olds know how to go on a diet, a survey by childcare professionals has found.

Weight worries start at pre-school, experts warned as research by the Professional Association for Childcare and Early Years (PACEY) showed almost a third of nursery and school staff have heard a child label themselves fat. Ten per cent said they had heard a child say they felt ugly. (You can learn more here: https://www.pacey.org.uk/news-and-views/news/archive/2016-news/august-2016/children-as-young-as-3-unhappy-with-their-bodies/)

"By the age of three or four some children have already pretty much begun to make up their minds (and even hold strong views) about how bodies should look" (Harding, J. PACEY).

The same study also found that there is evidence to suggest that some 4-year-olds are aware of strategies for how to lose weight and that around one in five children has also rejected food because "it will make them fat".

This followed research completed in 2019 by the London School of Hygiene and Tropical Medicine, King's College London and Harvard, that suggested children over the age of eight were displaying signs they were dissatisfied with their bodies.

(You'll find a report on this research here: https://www.telegraph.co.uk/news/2016/08/30/children-as-young-as-three-have-body-image-issues-while-four-yea/)

The YMCA conducted a study in May 2016. Major findings within their "Somebody Like Me" research included:

- 52% of 11 to 16 year olds regularly worry about how they look
- 30% of 11 to 16 year olds isolate themselves because of body image anxiety
- 36% of 11 to 16 year olds said they would do 'whatever it takes' to look good, including considering cosmetic surgery. (https://www.ymca.org.uk/wp-content/uploads/2017/01/Somebody_like_me-v1.0.pdf)

In 2021 Parnell et al. conducted a study that looked into the attitudes and friendship behaviours towards socially stigmatised appearances in children, aged four to 10, using their responses to characters. They found that the attitudes towards the different characters differed significantly.

The digitally designed characters had similar facial features and had these appearances:

- No stigmatised appearance,
- Wearing glasses,
- A higher weight,
- Had a facial burn,
- Was in a wheelchair.

The children had less positive attitudes and friendship behaviours towards the higher weight character and the characters with a facial burn and in a wheelchair.

I don't know about you, but I find all of this heart breaking, but not surprising.

Have a think about the TV and films you watch. How many of them have characters that are in larger bodies? How many have visible differences? How many of them are "goodies"? How many are "baddies"? How many of them are the heroes? The love interest? The academic?

Do the same with books that you read. Think about the advertisements you see, too.

How many representations of people who are not slim and able bodied do you see in the media? On social media?

Is it surprising that many children develop the impression that people who look different to them are not "friendship material"?

Then, add in the messages that they may be getting at home.

Caregivers who frequently talk about their bodies send a message that physical appearance is important. When they talk about their bodies with dissatisfaction, children come to believe that feeling bad about their bodies is the norm, putting them at higher risk for developing similar feelings about their own bodies.

Think of the language you use. Saying, "I hope you'll be taller than me", or, "I hope you don't end up like me", makes children feel you don't value you, that being like you would be awful, and that, if they aren't taller, or they are like you, that they aren't good enough either.

When we verbalise our perceived flaws, it teaches that it's not the "whole package" that matters. It teaches them to pick themselves apart and find what they think are their flaws. We teach them to imagine that other people look at them and only see those "flaws". And we teach them to not trust their own judgement on what beauty really is — *I think Mum is beautiful, but Mum says she has all these things wrong with her; Mum says she is always right, so am I wrong?*

Activities (write your answers in a notebook)

• What body "rules" were you brought up with? Knowing why you think the way you do will help you make conscious choices in the messages you send to your children.

• How many of them do you still believe?

• How many of them do you say to the children in your life?

• What about other members of your family? What do they say? To you? To your children?

• What language do you use around the children in your life? Think about when you are looking at your body/eating/trying on clothes.

How do you feel about your answers to those questions?

Does anything need to change?

We want to give our children and young people a confident start to life so that they can achieve everything they want to. We know that low body confidence and self-esteem can affect children at a young age, so it's vital that we start tackling it early.

If you're a parent, grandparent, aunt, uncle, brother, sister, friend, or teacher, you can affect the way the children in your life think about their bodies.

If you have responsibility for a child, ensure you set a positive example and encourage body confidence by using positive and avoiding negative language about your own body image or that of others.

- Use positive and inspiring language to encourage people to be body confident.

- Use messages that prioritise general well-being over just appearance and weight.

- Encourage people to have realistic and healthy aspirations.

- Talk about kindness, to ourselves and others.

- Don't say negative things about other people's bodies.

- Demonstrate a healthy relationship with your body.

- Don't use food as reward or punishment; don't say just sweets, chocolates and cakes are treats; include tasty fruit, story times, games, and other things.

- Demonstrate how moving your body can be fun; don't talk about calorie burning.

- Remind them how incredible our bodies are, not for what they look like but for what they do.

- Accept compliments, especially from and around your children.

- Make an effort to point out what's good about your body in front of your children, even if you don't necessarily believe it; treating your body well is good for you and them. Say something good about yourself, about your body, every day in front of your children. It's important your children know they can see their good points too.

- Fake it until you make it.

- And always be their ally. If someone else makes a negative comment about your child, counteract it. Also, agree with positive things others have said.

Have "Let's remind ourselves how brilliant we are" days! Have a list of prompts as reminders; here are a few I use:

1. I like myself because:

2. I'm really good at:

3. I am important because:

4. I'm a good friend because:

5. I am successful because:

6. I do well at school/work because:

Please do add your own.

You could also list all the ways that you are all beautiful, inside and out. Remember that there is no set type of beauty. There are so many ways a person is beautiful: their intelligence; their kindness; their smile; their heart. Beauty is inside and out.

List some ways you, and the people you love, are beautiful on the inside and out.

You could all start a self-esteem journal, as they are a great way to begin thinking about all the good things that you do and experience, which sets everyone up to view life more positively. You could decide you'll all do it for a week, or a month, or longer, and discuss what you have found.

Here are some prompts you can use — you could pick two or three to do every day (they don't have to be the same questions every day; indeed, it's more beneficial if you ask more questions so you can see how wonderful you are):

- Today, I enjoyed …
- Today, I did this well …
- Today, I felt happy when…
- Today, I felt proud when …
- Today, I achieved this …
- Today, I helped someone…
- Today was interesting because…
- Today, I loved it when …

- Today, I felt good about myself when…
- Today, I feel grateful because …

Create a kindness wall! I love a kindness wall!

Write loving, kind messages on Post-it notes and leave them around mirrors or have a wall that the whole family goes past every day. The notes can either stay where they are or be put in a pocket to be looked at as needed through the day.

Here are some ideas:

- You are strong!
- You are clever!
- You are funny!
- You are kind!
- You are loving!
- Your smile makes me happy.
- I love it when you sing.
- You make the best cookies.
- I love when we have fun together.
- You are such a good listener!
- Thank you for being you.

Please note how these aren't about physical appearance; you can add those, too, but if we only compliment someone on how they look, that's where their focus will be. One parent I worked with was very concerned about how thin their teenager was getting; I suggested putting positive notes around mirrors and in school bags/books/hidden in cupboards. They said they did that already; they then told me that, because they, understandably, wanted their child to feel good about how they looked, and not be concerned about their weight, their messages were all about how they looked. The parent had wonderful, loving intentions, but to their teen, it was more pressure to look good, whatever good meant for them. So, leave notes saying how beautiful they are, because they are, but leave far more that say how fantastic they are, just by being themselves.

My whole life has pretty much been about being who I needed; for the children in your life, please don't repeat behaviours that you have seen, that have upset you; **be who you needed**.

Chapter Twenty–Six

Bumblebee

"Aerodynamically the bumblebee shouldn't be able to fly, but the bumblebee doesn't know that so it goes on flying anyway."
— *Mary Kay Ash*

As a lot of what I do is about kindness, the next few chapters are about adding more of that into our lives. We all like to think we are kind but, sometimes, life gets in the way, or we feel out of our depth, and we don't know what to say or do. I'm hoping some of the following will help you feel more confident in believing you are just the friend someone needs.

I look healthy. I look robust. I'm even prone to bouts of energetic activity, especially on a dance floor, or when playing with children, or when I am at my favourite place, Monkey World.

I don't look disabled.

Unless I am using my stick, you cannot see that I may have difficulties moving around.

And, sometimes, when I am using a stick, you might see me participate in some behaviours that may seem peculiar and at odds with it. For example, those bobbly bits before crossings, they are brilliant for visually impaired people to know when they are approaching a road. For me, they are really painful on my already fragile feet, so, you might see me hobbling along, using my stick, then see me leap like a gazelle (that's how I look in my head, anyway) over them.

Thanks to my EB I'm prone to blistering and shearing on my hands, feet, mouth and throat (you can read more about it in chapter 16, 'Courage and strength'). Each of the conditions I discussed in part on is an invisible disability. A person would not know I have them unless I told them.

This can make things difficult. I would imagine that, for most of us who live with disabilities, things are more difficult than for those that don't.

As a business owner, which often includes organising events, I understand how difficult it is to be fully inclusive, to include every possible consideration for making an event accessible. But that doesn't mean I shouldn't try at all. This goes for both public and private events; many venues are difficult to access, whether it's for a fancy networking event, or for Uncle Bob's 60th.

That hotel surrounded by a natural forest is truly stunning! It's a beautiful setting for any kind of event. As the event organiser, you probably drove there, looked around, loved everything, great parking.

But what about the attendees who are unable to drive? How could they get there? That beautiful hotel in the middle of a forest is unlikely to be accessible via public transport, especially if it's not in the centre of a town. Maybe there's a bus that stops ten minutes' walk away. Great. If your mobility is good.

For me, to get to anywhere like that would usually involve at least two buses, possibly a train, and a walk, which would all take at least twice as long as someone driving in their car. And there are the elements to deal with as well. So, for me to get up and get somewhere like that, would mean leaving my house, hoping I won't get caught in wind or rain, hoping no buses or connections are delayed, being jostled on buses, then walking, possibly up uneven ground. I'm exhausted before I have even reached the event. Then, after hours of schmoozing, the journey has to be repeated in reverse. So, for a two hour meeting, for example, it would involve at least three hours of travelling time, and me being exhausted and unable to work or do anything else for the rest of the day and possibly the next day or two as well.

So how can you, as a wonderfully considerate human, make things easier?

Ask!! And listen to the answers.

Know that one size does not fit all; know that every day is different, even for those of us who live with the conditions.

I understand that you wouldn't want to change the venue, so make plans instead. Organise lift shares. Yes, the person who needs the lift could ask, but, one, as the organiser, you have more power, and, two, for the person with disabilities, it can be so demoralising to have to ask, to have to explain, over and over, why they are unable to drive. As the organiser, you can start a thread, or send messages, and say to anyone from this area please travel together if possible. You can say it's an environmental effort; why use four cars with one person in each, when you can use one car with four people in?

In addition to this, offer to get drinks and bring them to the table. Don't make events all standing. Don't judge us on how you see us at one time; as I mentioned at the beginning, I can have huge bursts of energy; other times I can struggle to walk.

For bigger events, especially ticketed ones, consider the venue. Is it accessible by public transport? Does it have lift access? Are the seats tiered? Tiered means steps, which aren't always accessible by everyone. Is there good leg room?

All of these things would be things that need to be considered for someone with most kinds of mobility difficulties. For me, having to walk up steps can cause additional pain; sitting in seats where I can't move my legs causes additional pain. It's also not too pleasant for people seated around me if I start spasming because of the excessive pain.

Other things to consider:

• Are there signs and information written in large print or braille?

• Are there ramps?

• Do entrance buttons work?

• Are corridors and doors wide enough for wheelchairs?

• Are there comfortable chairs? Stools are generally not good.

• Are there wheelchair accessible bathrooms? A Changing Places bathroom is even better!

For those people attending who are neurodiverse, who have mental health conditions, who have sensory issues, or are introverted, here are ways you can make your event more accessible:

• ensure there are quiet spaces for them to retreat to if they need to;

• ensure all material is accessible, whether that be in braille, in large print, or in audio format;

• ensure that seats aren't packed in so that people who need to can get up and walk around — this is also useful for some of us with mobility issues; I frequently "pace" when I am somewhere, as moving continuously can be less painful than sitting in a small space.

Most of all, let people know that you are a safe person to ask for support for their needs. When I put on unreserved ticketed events, I will ask for people to contact me if they need to sit by a door, near a bathroom, at the end of an aisle, or for any other needs they have.

Do you want your attendees to go away feeling uncomfortable, pained, and not having enjoyed the event, or go away knowing that you made every effort to be inclusive?

These things don't just apply to events. They apply to everyday living, too. If you can, when you arrange to meet a friend, offer to pick them up; unless you drive like a *Top Gear* presenter, it's far less exhausting to be a passenger in a car that you get in outside your front door, than it is to be walking to and waiting for buses. If you want to go out for day trips, think about the venue and if it is accessible; understand that some days when you go together, you may be cavorting through the daisies, and, other times, your friend may need an arm to hold on to. If you want to go for a picnic, think about if there are tables and chairs, so that your only option isn't just to sit on the ground; toilets are important, too. Please, just ask, listen, and learn.

Have you heard about the Spoon Theory? It says that those of us who live with chronic conditions only have so many spoons a day. Imagine we have 12 spoons a day.

Some days, we can use just one spoon for an event; other days, whether it's due to lack of sleep, higher levels of pain, exhaustion from the previous day's activities, or because you are fighting off an infection (which is quite frequently in my case, as it doesn't take much for blisters to get infected), it can take a spoon to just sit up and get out of bed.

Making breakfast can take another spoon. Having a shower and getting dressed can take another two spoons. That's four spoons before you have even left the house. Waiting for buses or other public transport, another spoon; travelling, another spoon; walking, another spoon; chatting to people (an enjoyable activity but it can be exhausting!) can be another spoon; travelling home, which is now harder because you are more tired, will be at least double the spoons, which is six spoons. The mathematicians amongst you will have worked out that that is 14 spoons. Which means you are already in deficit for the rest of the day, the next day, and possibly beyond.

You can make all of our social experiences together much easier and that would be very much appreciated.

And always remember that before we are anything else, we are all human, with the same thoughts and feelings as each other, and that we want to live life as fully as you do, whenever our disabilities allow. Please don't judge, and please don't make assumptions.

Chapter Twenty-Seven

Language

"But if thought corrupts language, language can also corrupt thought." — *George Orwell*

I want to talk about the language we use. This is another way in which you can be more inclusive and kinder, to yourself and others.

I will focus on the self-talk, before moving on to language more generally.

What words and phrases do you say to yourself when talking? Are they words of joy, positivity, and encouragement? Or are they critical, unkind, unforgiving?

Are you aware of saying them? How do those words make you feel?

I feel I have a slight advantage with being aware of my negative self-talk. You see, on the rare occasion I am not being kind to myself, I have noticed that I refer to myself by my birth name; probably because she had so few kind things said to her that it's now my go to name when I am being mean to myself. When I notice myself saying it, I can immediately start challenging the cruel things I am saying and bring myself back to being more Vie.

Think about the language you use when you talk to yourself, the language you use when you are talking about yourself.

How many kind words do you hear?

Or are you mostly critical about yourself? I would like you to challenge those critical thoughts.

As I've mentioned elsewhere in the book (chapter 20, 'A lifelong romance'), start being aware of all the incredible things your body does and thank it frequently.

And there's other things you can do.

Instead of telling yourself, and others, that you've been a lazy bitch all day because you've done nothing but sit on the sofa all day, change it! You weren't being lazy! You were taking much needed rest. And it's highly unlikely that your brain stopped, so you probably still thought about things you have to do, and work, and the family, and so on.

Instead of telling yourself, and others, that you were really greedy because you had a bag of crisps and a bar of chocolate for lunch, change it! You probably had those things to eat because you were rushing and that's all you had time for; or you're so tired, that's all you had the energy for. Don't criticise yourself for doing what you need to just to get through the day.

When you're in a shop and your hips or boobs bump into a display, do not tell yourself that it's because you take up too much space; remind yourself that shops cram in as much as possible, and that they are not leaving space for most people — people with hips, people in wheelchairs, people with pushchairs — to walk around without bumping into it. I wouldn't be surprised if there's some theory behind it, that people who knock things off of displays are more likely to buy out of embarrassment. You deserve to take up space! Take up as much as you want!

Also think about the words you say about others.

I read somewhere, a few years ago, that when we make judgements about others, our first thoughts are what we were brought up with and the second thought is who we are.

I shall give you an example. One day I was in a stationery and book shop; there was a young girl kneeling on the floor, stacking shelves. Her bottom cleft and some of her cheek were visible above her trousers. My first thought:

She's too big for those trousers!

My second thoughts:

Hang on. That's not me. This might be her first day on the job so she may not be able to afford to buy new trousers, so she is using ones from years ago, or that she has had to borrow. Or maybe she has started taking medication that has made her weight increase. Or maybe she tore her trousers on the way into work and these were the only size available left to wear.

Those thoughts that came after my first were far kinder.

When you think those mean thoughts about others, challenge them. Do you really believe them? Are they representing an insecurity in you that you are projecting onto them? What could be kinder words to use?

When you say those negative thoughts out loud, whether they are about yourself or someone else, what effect does it have? How does it make you feel? Who is listening? Who could you be affecting? Who could you be hurting?

I am far from perfect, and I do sometimes love a good moan, but most of the time, I try to channel my inner Thumper from *Bambi*: if you can't say nothing nice, don't say nothing at all.

There's also the language we use without thinking too much that can be troublesome.

So much of what is common vernacular, that many of us think nothing of saying because we believe we have no ill intent, is hurtful and damaging.

This could include sayings that are racist, sexist, homophobic, or ageist. All of our language needs to be considered, and it's a vast subject.

What I will focus on here is ableist language, as that is, thus far, the one I have most experience with.

As I've said, my conditions are, mostly, invisible, so when people see me, they see a woman, usually in a pretty frock, with flowers in her hair, being happy and enthusiastic. Some will make judgements about my size, or about my abundant grey hairs. Others will notice my energy and my smile. But they don't see my disabilities. Just like they don't see the disabilities millions of other people are living with.

The language people use is often discriminatory and dismissive towards people living with any health conditions. They probably won't be aware that their words are indicating their beliefs; they would probably believe that they are very kind and considerate when they meet someone who lives with a disability.

I thought I would share some of the things I've heard; some weren't directed at me, because they didn't know I have disabilities; others were.

In the introductory session of a networking meeting, we were asked to talk about what we like, what we enjoy; lovely! I thought.

Several people said that they value their health, which is great, as it has great value, then they followed it up with:

Without my health, I have nothing.

I. Have. Nothing.

What this says to me is that if we're not healthy, we can't have full, rich lives. We can't have fun or excitement. We can't have love and adventures.

Because, without health, "I have nothing".

This devalues my life and the life of every human that cannot be classed as healthy because of the nature of our conditions.

"I have nothing" tells me that you don't think my life is worth living because I am not healthy.

I. Have. Nothing.

This means that having a partner who loves and adores me means nothing.

This means all the lives I have had a positive impact on mean nothing.

This means all the fun and adventures I have mean nothing.

Now, when someone says, "Without my health, I am nothing", I have no doubt that they don't mean to imply all that, but they do. I have no doubt that they have probably not thought about that sentence much; they probably don't think about its implication. The thing is, so far, they haven't needed to, so they don't understand how hurtful it can be.

They probably also haven't thought about how fragile health can be. How, sometimes, in literally one moment, our health can be taken from us, through a random accident or incident; they don't think how likely it is that many of us will get cancer or dementia, or other life limiting conditions.

I want you to think about all you have in your life, all the people you love, all the things you enjoy, all the adventures you have. If your health was taken away from you, do those people mean less? Do you mean less to them? Does living mean less?

My value, your value, everyone's value, does not decrease in relation to how lacking in good health we are.

I've also been told by a few people that if I did this or that treatment, I would "feel more me".

In the words of the amazing song, "this is me"!!

I'm in pain every single second of every single day. There are things I struggle to do. There are things I can't do. A large part of the time, I'm beyond tired. I have to plan everything, right to planning I have the money, or a willing driver, to ensure I can get home from wherever I am in the country because my energy levels can change rapidly, as can my levels of pain. Without doubt, these things are difficult to live with.

But.

Through my illnesses, I have learned more about who I am. I have learned how strong I am. How determined I am. I have set myself challenges and surpassed them. I have had adventures I never could have dreamed of. I have people in my life I love. I run a business I am passionate about. I'm not healthy by many people's standards, but my life is full, full of love, kindness, and happiness.

And acceptance.

Acceptance of myself and everyone else.

Yes, I'm a person living with disabilities, but that is not all of who I am.

I am Vie; one of the kindest, happiest, most supportive, encouraging, loving, humans you are ever likely to meet.

This is who I am.

Chapter Twenty-Eight

Living on

"Those who have died live on the lips of the living" — *Gloria Hunniford*

I will admit that I haven't always been great at picking friends. I am, whether by nature or nurture, a rescuer, and that means I have often swooped in and tried to fix things, to make everything okay. And this has meant that many of my friendships have not been reciprocal. I am often wanted when they need something and ignored when things are going well for them, or if I am having a difficult time. Frequently, they also expect more from me than I am allowed to expect of them.

This was never more apparent than when several friends died in quick succession. As well as friends dying, many living friends disappeared too, because they weren't used to me needing support.

Grief is something we will all encounter in our lives; after all, we all know people, and we all know that people die, so it's obvious we will all deal with grief at some point. Hopefully, those times will be rare, but that may not necessarily be the case for all of us.

A lot of people in my life have died. Although my EB won't be the cause of my death, in its more severe forms, its complications can be fatal. Through this skin condition I am incredibly fortunate to know lots of other people with the condition; part of loving so many people with it means that we lose a lot of people too. It's always heart breaking, and no matter how many times it happens, it never, ever, gets easier.

There were a few years where three friends died. That's a lot. Then a couple of years ago, I lost five friends in the space of 11 months. Not just people I know, but people I have sat up late talking to; people I hugged when I saw them; people I have shared bits of me that many people don't see. Two of those people were two of my closest friends. Those two friends would be the friends I would be talking to now, sharing the excitements and worries about writing a book (both of them were talented writers, and they would be so pleased I am writing again!). But I can't. At least, I can't get a response from them when I do talk to them.

So, I know quite a bit about grief. I have supported people through it, and I have lived, am living, with it. But I know from experience that many people do not know how to be with someone who is grieving. As this part of the book is about encouraging people to be their best selves, I thought I would share some of my thoughts on how you can help someone who is grieving.

Grief, without exception, is hard, and, as with all feelings, it's important that everyone's emotions are heard and validated. There is no wrong way to grieve. We can all only do what it takes to get us through each day and hope that each day, it becomes easier to smile.

For those of you living with grief, whether directly or not, a theory that I have found so helpful, which is attributed to Lauren Herschel, is the ball in a box.

First, imagine that grief is a big ball that lives inside a box; also inside the box is a pain button; when you are first grieving, it is almost impossible to do anything without the ball hitting the pain button. However, over time, the ball gets smaller and it hits the pain button less often as it bounces around; but the pain button never gets lesser; every time the ball hits the button, the pain is still felt intensely. And, for me, that is grief; it never goes away, but you are overcome with it less and less frequently as time goes on. There's a link to a short video in the links section at the end of the book.

As it's been an all too regular occurrence, I have realised that most people do not know how to be around a grieving person. That could be because it's hard to be reminded of our own, or those we love's, mortality, or to be reminded of those we have already lost. It could be that although we will all encounter death, we have never learned how to respond effectively. It could be for many reasons.

You can read these and decide they are the wisest points ever, or that they are a pile of nonsense; you are entitled to have your opinion, just as I am to have mine, and these are what I would request of people wanting to support me.

1. The sympathetic head tilt.

Equally, saying, "Awwww".

This is not helpful. The intention behind it is understandable; it's done with kindness; however, all it demonstrates is that you don't know what to say.

It's okay to not know what to say. Say that! Say, "I don't know what to say but can I give you a hug?"

Say, "I don't know what to say but I would love for you to tell me about your friend."

We will never get to create new memories with the people we love who have died so it's really important to be able to talk about the memories we do have, so they remain part of our lives.

2. Show, don't tell.

During grieving periods, I have had lots of people tell me they love me. It's wonderful to feel that people love you, and it's very kind of people to say it. However, love is more than a word; it's an action. Don't tell people you love them then not ask how they are or offer to support them. Or, if you have so much going on in your life that you can't offer that, say that. Say, "I love you [person that is grieving], but, right now, I have no energy left to offer anyone, but when I see you, I will give you a big hug."

Maybe offer to go to the cinema together; that will show you want to spend time together and you'll have the film to talk about.

Grief is very lonely; showing someone you care by being there physically, even if you can't quite do it emotionally (as long as you have expressed that you don't have the emotional ability currently) will mean a lot. Be honest. Grief is a big thing for someone to carry, whether it's you feeling the grief or being the person to help carry it; if you don't have the strength to carry it, say so. If you just avoid the person grieving, they will believe you don't care and that will be another grief for them to deal with.

3. Listen.

Listen even when they are not saying anything.

If you text or phone and they don't respond, don't be annoyed; maybe they can't people right now. Text them (sometimes voicemails can feel intrusive) and say that you were just messaging to see how they are and that you will message again another day. They need to know you care and that you aren't angry that they can't communicate verbally right now. If you have messaged every day for a while (whatever that while means to you) and you have seen no signs of life, message and say that you are worried about them, that you know that they aren't up to talking, but please could they just tell you they are still alive, so you don't feel the need to go and knock down their front door.

Listen to what they are not saying.

We know that people sometimes aren't good at talking about feelings so, in true stiff upper lip fashion, we may go, "I'm fine" when asked how we are.

Most people who say they are fine are far from it. If someone says this to you, ask them another question that may get more of a response. Say, "You might not want to talk about it, and that's okay, but I am here to listen if you would like to tell me that you really aren't fine."

Listen to what they are saying.

If you have tried to get them to talk and they don't want to, and they have told you time and again they don't want to, believe them. But don't stop contacting them. Send texts, cards, gifts. Let them know that although they may not want to talk, you still care.

If they do talk, listen with the intent of hearing, not responding; don't interrupt.

If you can't comprehend the pain they are in, or what they are saying, again, be honest, say that. Tell them that what they are saying is beyond your understanding right now, but goodness! It all sounds incredibly hard, and that you may not have words of wisdom, but you can offer a hand to hold.

It's okay to not understand every emotion someone else has but it's important that if someone is sharing it with you, you listen with kindness.

4. Don't say, "Call me if you need anything".

It's understandable why people say this. We feel we are helping. But it's also a way of putting more responsibility on the person grieving. That person is already struggling; they may not know what they want or need; they may not know how to ask for it.

They may think you don't mean it, that it's just a platitude; and they already have too much to think about.

Instead, offer suggestions.

Ask if they need anything when you do a supermarket shop.

Ask if they would like to meet for a coffee and a chat; tell them you would like to know more about the person they are grieving because they were obviously wonderful for people to be grieving them, but that you are also equally happy to sit in silence, reading books over a hot chocolate and a slice of cake.

Keep inviting them to things; they may say no, but it will be important for them to feel included.

Offer specific things, not just general comments. Take responsibility to be their friend and help them. Ensure they know you expect nothing of them. If they say they need teabags when you are shopping, ask if they would prefer it for you to leave them on the doorstep, so they know you aren't expecting a conversation, but that you are happy to chat if they would like to.

This point, especially, is also good if you are supporting a friend with a terminal illness. A person who has a terminal condition, nearing the end of life, needs love, support, and consideration, and they are frequently overwhelmed with needing to ensure everyone they are leaving behind is coping. Offer all the same things. For example, you're going shopping, ask if they need anything, and listen to what they need. Also, a person who is nearing the end of life might want to see people but might get exhausted quickly; ask them how long it takes before they start to feel that way. Then visit and set your alarm so you don't stay longer than they can cope with, so if they say it takes 15 minutes before they are utterly exhausted, set your phone timer for ten minutes. Offer to give feet and hand massages; by this point, a lot of the touching they receive is medicalised, with blood tests, injections, tubes; simply by rubbing their hands and feet, possibly in silence, you are showing them affection and that you value them as a human, and not a pin cushion. If they love to read but are struggling to do that, offer to read to them, or record yourself reading and send them the recording so they can listen when they feel able.

And remember that this is not about you; it's about supporting them.

5. Remember that the funeral doesn't always give closure.

Funerals, although tear-inducing affairs, can also be quite wonderful. They are a chance to say a public goodbye and spend a few hours talking to people who also loved the person you are grieving for, without feeling that you are boring them.

However, the next morning, and many mornings after that, when they wake up, the grief is still there. Respect that. Continue to treat the person tenderly until they have demonstrated to you that, although their grief will always be a part of them, they are now back to their variation of normal. You will know whether they are faking it because you will have shown by now how great a friend you are by following the previous points.

6. Think about the language you use around the person grieving.

In our current vernacular, we use words that, in their true meaning, have such depth and power, but they have been used to mean something less. Think about those words. Think about what you are going to say before you say it. Don't say that you feel so poorly you feel like you are dying, when you know you are not; just say you feel really rough. Don't say you are dying for a cup of tea; just say you are desperate for a cuppa instead.

Often, those words will slide over the listeners because they are so much part of our language now, but to someone already feeling surrounded by death, those words can be jarring.

7. Don't make assumptions.

Just because your grieving friend is out wearing neon, clubbing until dawn, don't assume they are "okay now". Maybe they are, but maybe they are out dancing to trance to block out the noises in their head, throwing back vodka because it numbs the pain. Ask them how they are. Refer to point 3 and listen to their answer, the one coming from their mouth and their actions.

Just because your friend is "carrying on as normal", don't assume that anything feels normal to them. Understand that they may have a job to do, and they still need to get paid. Understand that they may need to be occupied with something else.

Don't assume that because your friend is grieving, they don't want to be included. Maybe, what they really need is to be surrounded by friends as you all go and scream at a boy band or at a rally. Still invite them to things, even if they keep saying no. Ensure they know that you still care and that you still want their company, even if they are currently only capable of crying and monosyllabic utterances.

Don't assume that because they are smiling and laughing, there isn't still pain. Life is full of so many emotions, and, hopefully, we are all capable of feeling more than one of them in a day.

Don't assume you know what they are feeling.

8. Treat others as you want to be treated.

This is an adage that many of us claim to live by, yet, in many circumstances, we will expect things of some people that we would not expect from ourselves, and we do things that, in similar circumstances, we wouldn't want done to us.

When you have a grieving person in your life, think about how you would like to be treated. Think about what you would like your friends to do, what you would like help with, what you would need. Then be that person to the person who needs you right now.

And please remember that grief isn't just felt when a human dies.

A person could be grieving when a beloved pet dies.

They could be grieving the family they never had.

They could be grieving an item that had sentimental value.

They could be grieving a car or an item of clothing that always made them feel safe but that has broken.

They could be grieving the life they wanted but could never have.

Listen. Be kind. Be loving. Be supportive. Be honest.

And always remember that there is no right or wrong way to grieve.

Chapter Twenty-Nine

PositiVIEty

I often say that my head lives in a musical; I nearly always have a song in my head when I wake up in the morning, and others will pop in and out as the day progresses. Other songs, triggered by words or actions of others, will also join in. Music has always been really important to me; as a child, it gave me the escapism I craved, through words, through dance, and those times felt like rare times of safety and happiness; as an adult, music has represented my growth and been in my head for every big thing I have done.

Here are a selection of the songs that my brain often reverts to singing, and, sometimes, the rest of me joins in, too. It will be obvious why some of them are here; for example, the astounding "This Is Me", sung by the amazing Keala Settle in *The Greatest Showman*. My partner and I saw Hugh Jackman perform on his 2019 tour in the UK, which was incredible! Keala Settle came on stage to sing, and almost everyone around us, from the nine-year-old girl in front of us, to the older woman next to us, and me, joined in loudly and passionately; this song resonated with us all. There were tears; it was beautiful.

Others may not be so obvious. But, have a listen; sing along; see how you feel. And please feel free to add your own to the list, too. I would love it if you shared them with me; just find me on social media under VieNessCIC.

Petula Clark: "Colour My World"[1] and "Downtown"[2]

Cyndi Lauper said that "On my darkest days, I wear my brightest colours". There have been days when I didn't want to wear my usual colourful clothes; I think of this quotation and put on something bright and cheery; it always brightens my mood and reminds me that I have achieved so much, overcome so much, so I can get through the bad day. The song, "Colour My World", sung by Petula Clark, often pops into my head when I am thinking about colour, clothes, and what I am going to wear; these few lines in particular:

So you can colour my world

With sunshine yellow each day

Oh you can colour my world

With happiness all the way

Another Petula Clark favourite of mine is "Downtown", which I've already mentioned in this, but I cannot express its importance to me enough. This is the song that I danced to, that I often cried to, in my bedroom as a child, and frequently as an adult, that gave me hope. It made me believe that someday, somewhere, my people will be waiting for me; that the loneliness I felt would pass. Thankfully, it did.

Helen Reddy: "I Am Woman"[3]

I really couldn't tell you why I know this song, "I Am Woman", sung by Helen Reddy, but it has felt really important for a very long time. Whenever I am about to do something scary, something anxiety inducing, such as public speaking or performing, I listen to this, and I am bolstered! I remind myself of all the much scarier things I have done, all the things I have overcome, the things I have learned, and I am ready! Bring it on!

Fairground Attraction: "Find My Love" [4]

Again, I have mentioned this song, Fairground Attraction's "Find My Love", previously. Another song of hope; a song that helped me believe that, one day, I would be loved and accepted. It happened; I am loved and accepted. And the following lyrics in particular helped me believe that I wasn't the only one like me, living through what I was:

There must be someone

There must be someone like me

Sittin' lonely as a boat out there

It also reminds me of this affirming quotation from Frida Kahlo: "I used to think I was the strangest person in the world but then I thought there are so many people in the world, there must be someone just like me who feels **bizarre** and flawed in the same ways I do."

Shirley McClain: "If They Could See Me Now" [5]

Although a large part of this song, "If They Could See Me Now", sung by Shirley McClain, isn't relevant, it does go through my mind when I am about to do something that the friends I had in my earlier years would never believe I would do; that I never believed I could do! I've had friends from school message me and say they are very surprised about things I have done, the things I do, because the quiet me they knew would never have done them. Sometimes, when I am about to do something most people don't, these lines are in my head:

All I can say is, wow

Hey, look at where I am

I've landed, pow

Right in a pot of jam

This was going to be the song I made my burlesque debut to, because it felt so bizarre to think of what I was doing, but I changed it to something else.

Julie Andrews: "I Have Confidence" [6]

This song, from *The Sound Of Music* is actually not my favourite song from the musical; my favourite song is "The Lonely Goatherd". I love a good (attempt at a) yodel! However, this song, "I Have Confidence", sung by Julie Andrews, goes through my head when I sometimes feel I need a boost. I particularly like the lines when she is sharing her confidence in sunshine, rain, and spring, then in herself; it reminds me to find the good in the day, because there is always good somewhere.

My brain is on permanent shuffle, and it usually finds the song I need at the right time.

Kela Settle: "This Is Me" [7]

"This Is Me", sung by Keala Settle in *The Greatest Showman* is such a powerful song! I, along with probably many millions of others, feel this in my heart; when she sings of being broken and scarred, of being told you are unlovable, then to share we are truly glorious, wow! I feel it! If you have read the rest of the book, it will be fairly obvious why this song resonates. I am no longer ashamed of my scars. This really is me.

Elvis Presley: "If I Can Dream" [8]

"If I Can Dream" is my favourite Elvis song. There are lots of his that I love to dance to and sing along with, but this is the one that means the most.

When I start doubting that the world is mostly good, I listen to this song loudly. It reminds me that there is good in the world; it reminds me that I believe in being the change I want to see; it reminds me that there is so much we can dream of and achieve.

And, with these lyrics,

And while I can think, while I can talk

While I can stand, while I can walk

While I can dream

I am reminded of the Martin Luther King quotation: "If you can't fly then run, if you can't run then walk, if you can't walk then crawl, but whatever you do you have to keep moving forward." I believe we are all here to make a difference and this song, this quote, prompts me to remember that when things feel hopeless.

Sara Bareilles: "Brave" [9]

Whenever you are feeling overwhelmed by a past or current hurt, I urge you to listen to Sara Bareilles' song, "Brave". I just love it! I see it as an anthem. The video is great, too. I never considered myself brave until this last decade or so; I'm very grateful I have been. How have you been brave? What does *brave* mean to you?

P!nk: "All I Know so Far!" [10]

"All I Know so Far!" By P!nk is a last minute addition, as it's only recently been released. When I heard this song it felt like me (though I have never been a spitter). Another really powerful song that resonates. It reminds me that, although I felt so very alone, there are too many others who have felt the same. If you have lived a life anything like mine, I really hope this song boosts you, and I really hope my story has made you feel less alone.

1. Source: LyricFind Songwriters: Tony Hatch / Jackie Trent Colour My World lyrics © Sony/ATV Music Publishing LLC.

2. Source: Musixmatch Songwriters: Hatch Anthony Peter Downtown lyrics © Emi Blackwood Music Inc., Welbeck Music Ltd., Smack Hits, Sony/atv Story Music Publishing, Warner/Chappell Music Ltd.

3. Source: Musixmatch Songwriters: Ray Burton / Helen Reddy I Am Woman lyrics © Buggerlugs Music Co., Irving Music, Inc.

4. Source: Musixmatch Songwriters: Nevin Mark Edward Cascian Find My Love lyrics © Mca Music Ltd.

5. Source: LyricFind Songwriters: Cy Coleman / D. Fields If My Friends Could See Me Now lyrics © Words & Music A Div. of Big Deal Music LLC.

6. Source: Songwriters: Richard Rodgers I Have Confidence lyrics © Williamson Music

7. Source: Songwriters: Justin Paul / Benj Pasek This Is Me lyrics © Sony/ATV Music Publishing LLC, Kobalt Music Publishing Ltd., DistroKid

8. Written by Earl Brown Publishers Gladys Music, Inc.

9. Source: Songwriters: Jack Antonoff / Sara Bareilles Brave lyrics © Sony/ATV Music Publishing LLC.

10.   Source: Songwriters: Alecia Moore / Benj Pasek / Justin Paul All I Know So Far lyrics © Sony/ATV Music Publishing LLC.

Chapter Thirty

A whole woman

"Stepping onto a brand-new path is difficult, but not more difficult than remaining in a situation, which is not nurturing to the whole woman." — Maya Angelou

Thank you for reading my story.

I know some bits may have been harrowing (if you need help or guidance, please do reach out; there are support numbers in the back of the book), but I hope that, overall, you have come away with feelings of hope, joy, encouragement, and love.

My life has been difficult, even brutal, more often than it has been happy, but the important thing is that it's happy now.

I hope my story has shown you that we can overcome so many things, starting with one single step of bravery. I hope my story has shown you that although we may often feel we are the only ones going through something, there are others who will understand.

I cannot change my past, just as you can't change yours, but everything that has happened has helped shape who I am, and I like who I am now.

And I am grateful I am here.

I would like you to do something for me. I would like you to always remember that you are wonderful, and to encourage you to always be your own kind of beautiful.

Vie

xx

"You deserve the best, the very best, because you are one of the few people in this lousy world who are honest to themselves, and that is the only thing that really counts." – Frida Kahlo

"Feet, what do I need you for when I have wings to fly?" — Frida Kahlo

Chapter Thirty-One

Support

There have been quite a lot of triggering topics in this book. If you feel you need help and support, please do reach out to friends, family, your local GP, local organisations, or any of the organisations below.

As I said at the beginning of the book, any trauma is bad, whether it's a one off incident or several years worth, and everything in between. You deserve support. You deserve kindness. Please don't be alone in this.

Miscarriage

Miscarriage Association
https://www.miscarriageassociation.org.uk/

Grief

Cruse
https://www.cruse.org.uk/

Abuse

Rape Crisis
https://rapecrisis.org.uk/

Yellow Door
https://yellowdoor.org.uk/

Victim Focus
https://www.victimfocus.org.uk/

https://childline.org.uk/ 0800 1111

Domestic Abuse

Yellow Door
https://yellowdoor.org.uk/

Women's Aid
https://www.womensaid.org.uk/

Victim Focus
https://www.victimfocus.org.uk/

Dragonfly Project
https://www.facebook.com/YOUDragonflyProject/

Narcissism

The Echo Society
https://www.theechosociety.org.uk/about

Counselling

Counselling DIrectory
https://www.counselling-directory.org.uk/

Mental Health

Mind
https://www.mind.org.uk/
0300 123 3393

Frazzled Cafe
https://www.frazzledcafe.org/

Boys Get Sad Too
https://boysgetsadtoo.com/

Young Minds
https://www.youngminds.org.uk/

The Samaritans
https://www.samaritans.org
116 123

Rethink Mental Illness
https://www.rethink.org

CALM
https://www.thecalmzone.net/
0800 58 58 58

Papyrus Prevention of Young Suicide
https://papyrus-uk.org
0800 0684141

The Mix (for under 25)
https://www.themix.org.uk
0808 808 4994

Sane
https://www.sane.org.uk
0300 304 7000

The Hub of Hope
https://www.hubofhope.co.uk

MindOut (LGBTQ+)
https://www.mindout.org.uk

Shout Crisis Text Line - Text 85258

Epidermolysis bullosa support

Debra
https://www.debra.org.uk/

Resources and Recommendations

These are people and organisations that are wonderful to see in your newsfeed or emails. They are knowledgeable people, on all sorts of topics and they can also bring joy.

A Mindful Moment
https://www.youtube.com/watch?v=F6eFFCi12v8&t=41s

Action for Happiness
https://www.actionforhappiness.org/

Lindo Bacon
www.lindobacon.com

The Fat Doctor
www.fatdoctor.co.uk

VieNess Discover You Love You CIC
www.vieness.co.uk
@VieNessCIC

InStar Coaching
https://instarcoaching.com/

A Work In Progress podcast
https://anchor.fm/p-awip

Love Disfigure
https://instagram.com/love_disfigure?utm_medium=copy_link

The Disability Union
https://disabilityunion.co.uk/

Parallel Global
https://www.parallellifestyle.com/

The Amplified Dot
https://linktr.ee/theamplifiedot

Scarred not scared
https://instagram.com/scarrednotscared?utm_medium=copy_link

Virgie Tovar
https://www.virgietovar.com/

BodiPosiPanda
https://instagram.com/meganjaynecrabbe?
utm_medium=copy_link

Harnum Kaur
https://instagram.com/harnaamkaur?utm_medium=copy_link

Lizzi Howell
https://linktr.ee/lizzydances

Aiya Mayrock
https://www.aijamayrock.com/

Blair Imani
https://blairimani.campsite.bio/

Amanda Jette Knox
https://instagram.com/maven_of_mayhem?
utm_medium=copy_link

Anti Diet Riot Club
https://linktr.ee/antidietriotclub

Carly Findlay
https://linktr.ee/carlyfindlay

The Latest Kate
https://linktr.ee/thelatestkate

Juno Dawson
https://instagram.com/junodawson?utm_medium=copy_link

Songs

Petula Clark *Colour My World*
https://www.youtube.com/watch?v=oDO7HPqPwSg

Petula Clark *Downtown*
https://www.youtube.com/watch?v=z_m4Qb0iW-o

Helen Reddy *I Am Woman*
https://www.youtube.com/watch?v=rptW7zOPX2E

Fairground Attraction *Find My Love*
https://www.youtube.com/watch?v=gA2V7fIzoOY

Shirley McClain *If They Could See Me Now*
https://www.youtube.com/watch?v=NANKaS_86xU

Julie Andrews *I Have Confidence*
https://www.youtube.com/watch?v=JJYz8pyXOG4

Keala Settle *This Is Me*
https://www.youtube.com/watch?v=CjxugyZCfuw

Elvis Presley *If I Can Dream*
https://www.youtube.com/watch?v=u-pP_dCenJA

Sara Bareilles *Brave*
https://www.youtube.com/watch?v=QUQsqBqxoR4

P!nk *All I Know So Far*
https://www.youtube.com/watch?v=wGj9oADcyRs

9 781838 427443